"This cookbook is one you'll be reaching for time and time again when you need healthy food that is satisfying and delicious."
—TIEGHAN GERARD

"Liz does an amazing job helping you make delicious food in a way that is both feasible and fun."
—RACHEL MANSFIELD

"Liz's message is profound, yet so simple . . . you need to have both whole foods and whole, real relationships to truly be healthy and happy. This book makes eating healthy a celebration, not a sacrifice, and it brings an arsenal of fresh and flavorful recipes that are fun to make and eat!"
—JEANINE DONOFRIO

"*Healthier Together* focuses on real whole foods and bringing community together whether you feel like indulging, imbibing, or cleaning it up. It's all about a balanced lifestyle!"
—KELLY LEVEQUE

"Liz's recipes are simple, laid-back, and so freaking delicious. You'll want to jump into every page of this book and share these beautiful dishes with someone you love."
—JESSICA MURNANE

"Connection to food and connection to family and friends = community! Nothing beats cooking what you love with those you love, and Liz has nailed it with her collection of healthy and completely delicious recipes for every craving and occasion."
—JASMINE AND MELISSA HEMSLEY

Healthier Together

CLARKSON POTTER/PUBLISHERS
NEW YORK

Healthier Together

Recipes for Two—
Nourish Your Body,
Nourish Your Relationships

Liz Moody

Photographs by Lauren Volo

Published in the United States by Clarkson Potter/
Publishers, an imprint of the Crown Publishing Group,
a division of Penguin Random House LLC, New York.

crownpublishing.com

clarksonpotter.com

CLARKSON POTTER is a trademark and POTTER
with colophon is a registered trademark of Penguin
Random House LLC.

Library of Congress Cataloging-in-Publication Data
Names: Moody, Liz, author. | Volo, Lauren,
    photographer (expression)
Title: Healthier together : recipes for two—nourish
    your body, nourish your relationships / Liz Moody ;
    photographs by Lauren Volo.
Description: First edition. | New York: Clarkson Potter/
    Publishers, 2019. | Includes index.
Identifiers: LCCN 2018027627 (print) | LCCN 2018029339
    (ebook) | ISBN 9780525573289 |
    ISBN 9780525573272 (hardcover)
Subjects: LCSH: Cooking. | Dinners and dining. |
    Nutrition. | LCGFT: Cookbooks.
Classification: LCC TX714 (ebook) | LCC TX714.M6666
    2019 (print) | DDC 641.5—dc23
LC record available at http://lccn.loc.gov/2018027627

978-0-525-57327-2
Ebook 978-0-525-57328-9

Printed in China

Book design by Mia Johnson
Cover photography by Lauren Volo

10 9 8 7 6 5 4 3 2 1

First Edition

To Zack,

who makes me healthier
and happier every single day

Contents

Welcome to a Healthier, Happier Life

People often ask me what I eat. As someone who devotes her life to healthy food (I'm food writer/editor by day, and a wellness blogger and healthy cookbook author by night), it's a fair question. They're looking, I think, for inspiration, but also to assuage guilt: ideas for breakfast and assurance that cookies and a second glass of wine aren't that bad, really (and they're not!). I tell them about my daily staples and the little hacks I've developed for healthy eating. But I'll also tell them that food, while key, is only one part of the wellness puzzle. Oftentimes, those who struggle on their wellness journey have failed to consider the missing piece: the people with whom they choose to journey. Once this piece slides into place, a healthy, satisfying picture emerges.

Let me back up a little bit.

Growing up, I didn't have a great relationship with food. My parents got divorced when I was three. My mom, who lived in Arizona, viewed food as a necessary inconvenience in daily life. We ate boiled hot dogs and steamed salmon standing around our kitchen island, or, more often than not, we'd skip dinner altogether in favor of foraging up something satiating enough to tide us over. At my father's house, in California, my stepmother insisted on dinner as a time to gather; my half-sisters and I were expected to be at the table at 6 p.m. nightly to eat a traditional American meal (spaghetti with marinara sauce, roast chicken). While, in theory, it was a lovely practice, in reality, my stepmom and father were already deeply entrenched in the discord that would ultimately lead to their divorce. Most nights, we ate to the stress-inducing tune of forks clinking against plates, my sisters and I racing to see how quickly we could finish and make our exit from the tension-filled table.

I spent my high-school years seeking solace from my home life and the inevitable awkwardness of being a teenager in far too much comfort food, seizing my newfound Volkswagen Jetta–enabled independence as an opportunity to visit Cold Stone Creamery on a daily basis. I ate the cake batter ice cream by myself, in my car, and it provided sweet respite—until the bowl was empty. In my early college years, I overcompensated in the other direction with a mono-diet of steamed broccoli. I settled into a routine of calorie counting, filled with Lean Cuisines and high-fiber cereals, viewing food as a necessity—and a number to burn off on the elliptical machine. And then I met Zack.

Zack was raised in Berkeley, California, a place where health and flavor have long been synonymous. It was in Berkeley that Alice Waters, touted as the inventor of California cuisine and founder of the famous Chez Panisse, placed a peach on a plate and declared that it, by itself, constituted dessert. It's a town filled with professors and other people who spent the late '60s and '70s on communes and in tiny health food stores that have been around since way before kale was cool. On our second date, Zack made me kimchi and vegetable pancakes from a macrobiotic cookbook he'd found at a thrift store. He did this casually—he was not a crunchy hippie; in fact, he'd barbecued bacon for breakfast that morning. We sat on his tiny cement balcony in the balmy California February night and I nibbled at the colorful fritter, which, in both color and smell, was the polar opposite of the cardboard I'd grown accustomed to consuming. I took a bite and the sour, sweet, crunchiness exploded in my mouth. *This was food?* I took another bite and then another. I was in.

Food—*this* kind of food—became a backbone to our burgeoning relationship. Zack and I visited farmer's markets and tiny Mexican food stands and specialty grocery stores, where we sampled tart sourdough breads, single-origin chocolate bars, and sodas made from fennel, quince, and golden beets. We cooked for each other and we ate together and I became addicted—addicted to the way food could taste and the way it could make me feel. My energy, after I ditched the cardboard, was off the charts; my weight, after I stopped calorie counting, dropped and settled into an effortlessly stable place.

At our wedding years later, our guests dined under the stars on the best farm-to-table dishes I've ever had (you can try some of it yourself on page 97!). That day, and every day since, our commitment to nourishing ourselves and enjoying life with gusto have been inextricably entangled, and our life has benefitted immensely as a result.

I was writing a newspaper column at the time, which was syndicated across the country. The job afforded me the opportunity to indulge my newfound passion for food around the world. I took cooking classes in Italy, where I realized that there is no such thing as Italian food: there is Tuscan food and Roman food and Sicilian food, and all of it told a bite-by-bite history of the land and the people on it and the wars they fought and the people they loved. I'd drunk wine for years, but at a sommelier course in Paris, it somehow dawned on me that all wine—with notes ranging from moldy cheese to sweet caramel apples—came from the same food: grapes. Grapes that spoke of the people who picked them and a volcano that exploded hundreds of years ago and the way the sun shone particularly brightly one summer. In Jordan with my father, a kind man we encountered took us back to his house to meet his grandmother, who, he insisted, "loooved visitors." He'd used up his 10 English words by the time we got to the small tiled apartment, and his grandmother had none, but smiled broadly as she put out a plate full

of figs from her garden and fresh mint tea. We sat in near-silence, smiling at each other as the sticky fig juice dripped down our arms. When the grandson drove us back down the mountain, he was effusive. "She looooved you," he said. "She loved you so much." All we'd done was share a snack.

Food is the one thing that all people, in all cultures, have in common. We fall in love over food, we celebrate over food, and we mourn over food. Food has a power to bring us together like nothing else. Why can't we channel this power toward health? By and large, it is unhealthy food that strains these bonds. If you're grabbing fast food on the way home from work, you're often eating alone in your car. If you're buying a pint of ice cream to console yourself, you might not be calling the friend whose embrace and ability to say just the right thing will actually salve your soul. Why can't we be together and be healthier? The first step is making the commitment to get back into the kitchen and around the table with others, to the place where food and relationships have been nurtured into something deeply nourishing for centuries. That's the primary aim of this book—to get you in the kitchen with someone, whether it's a friend, a partner, a coworker, or a family member, and to get you cooking food that makes you look and feel amazing. If all you did was cook most of your food with a partner, you'd be taking drastic steps toward making your life healthier—and not just in the eating-lots-of-green-stuff way. You'll also be happier, which, to me, is the impetus for getting healthy in the first place.

Look—we all know we should eat better. We've all felt the blood sugar crash that comes after eating a bagel for breakfast, or the low-grade nausea after a few too many bites of fried food. You may have committed to eating healthier throughout your life, whether it was a New Year's resolution or inspiration from reading about a new celebrity diet. And it usually works—for a while. You eat your salads, you go to the gym, but all the while, you feel as if you're missing out, whether it's on your colleagues' postwork happy hour or your husband's burrito. But the secret is in the partner. When you get healthier *together*, there is no missing out. You and your coworker can make your own happy-hour bites (including wine and cocktails—see page 124!) that won't make you lethargic at the office the next day. You and your husband can hit up the local farmer's market before making a produce-packed meal and come away from a night spent laughing and feeding each other tastes more physically and romantically satisfying than a night spent on the couch with greasy take-out boxes on your laps. A recent study showed that people are far more likely to stick to a workout and diet plan when tackling it with a partner. There are also numerous studies about how much your friends' and partners' health choices influence you: if you surround yourself with healthy people, you're far more likely to be healthy yourself, and, unfortunately, the opposite of that is true as well. By picking a person (or people!) to be healthier together with, you form a bubble of protection that will help fortify your own good habits.

This is not a book about sacrifice. This is a book about strengthening your relationships through your healthy choices, and strengthening your healthy choices through your relationships. This book is about saying yes to your best life.

So What Does "Healthy" Mean Anyway?

One of the reasons people give up on trying to "eat healthy" before they even get started is that "healthy" is a really ambiguous and ever-changing label. It seems like new diets come and go on a monthly basis: first fat is the enemy, then coconut oil is a superfood; veganism is the ultimate healing diet, then it's paleo. As the food director at mindbodygreen, I work with some of the country's best integrative and functional medicine doctors, people like Dr. Vincent Pedre, Dr. Sara Gottfried, Dr. Will Cole, Dr. Frank Lipman, and more—and even they don't all agree about what constitutes a healthy diet.

As science makes strides, we're constantly discovering new parts of our bodies that food impacts. Several years ago, the concept of gut health made its way into the mainstream, as researchers crowed that the gut was the body's "second brain," and poor gut health—caused by environmental toxins, poor diets, chlorinated drinking water, and other common elements of modern life—was the culprit behind many autoimmune diseases, anxiety, depression, and more. More recently, mitochondria—cells that thrive on fat—have led the discussion. What's next? No one really knows—the landscape of health is always changing, which is one of the things that make it so exciting.

But where does that leave us? In creating the recipes here, I've drawn on the knowledge gleaned from the doctors I work with (you'll find their advice sprinkled throughout the book), ancient wisdom, healing modalities from around the world, and the latest in scientific research. The one thing every single doctor I work with agrees on? We all need to eat more vegetables. Much of this cookbook is devoted to celebrating vegetables and working them into every part of a dish possible. That doesn't mean that meat is absent from this book. After reading countless studies and interviewing hundreds of doctors, I came to the conclusion that eating meat is primarily an ethical choice. If you don't want to eat meat for ethical reasons, I completely respect that, and, as such, almost every recipe in this book is either naturally vegetarian or easily adapted to be so (with many also easily made vegan). I also believe the healthiest diets use meat almost as a condiment, rather than as the anchor of the plate, leaving room for more vegetables. If you do opt to include animal protein, I strongly encourage you to buy the best quality you can afford (and you should be able to afford better, since you're eating less of it!)—for the environment, the treatment of the animals, and the health of your own body.

At the end of the day, though, I thought Mark Sisson, the bestselling author, entrepreneur, and founder of the primal (a version of paleo) diet put it best. I asked him about studies that connected plant-based diets and longevity, such as that of the Okinawans and the Seventh-Day Adventist communities, which are referred to as "Blue Zones" because of their long-living populations. "We all agree on the vast majority of what we're eating," he explained. "Plants. Frankly, I think that last 15 percent we're all arguing about matters less than people think." He also added that he thinks the strong communities of the Blue Zones are as responsible for their long life spans as diet, if not more so. Another vote, then, for the importance of getting, and staying, healthier together.

I've also included ingredients and methodologies proven to help you feel better. Like many of the world's best functional medicine doctors, I believe that much of modern disease is rooted in inflammation and poor gut health (which, in turn, lead to each other), and, as such, many of the recipes in this book are designed to be strongly anti-inflammatory, and to help heal your gut by packing in pre- and probiotics while eliminating common irritants. I'll also teach you secret healing tricks, like how to use garlic to make it super–immune-boosting, how to feed your mitochondria the healthy fats that will keep your energy consistently high, and how to combine turmeric with black pepper to make the Ayurvedic staple more bioavailable.

One of the tenets of my healthy food philosophy revolves around keeping your blood sugar stable, and, in doing that, your hormones balanced. More and more, science points to the cascading negative health effects of imbalanced hormones, many of which are caused, at least in part, by the blood sugar spikes and falls that result from a standard American diet. These range from that 3 p.m. super-tired feeling to diabetes to thyroid and adrenal disorders and more. Keeping your blood sugar stable will help you stave off hunger, give you sustained energy throughout the day, and result in your craving better-for-you foods, making it way more likely you'll naturally not want to reach for that afternoon candy bar. Honestly—if you did nothing but eat food that kept your blood sugar stable and your hormones balanced, you'd be in pretty great shape from a health perspective. I do this by including a mix of healthy fat, fiber, and protein in every meal. For the same reasons, this book is completely free of refined sugars, relying instead on fiber-rich fruits, like dates and bananas, or lower–glycemic index (GI) sweeteners, like coconut sugar, to sweeten.

There are also no refined grains, including not just white flour, but also whole-wheat or spelt flour (both react only mildly differently in your body than white flour, and all of them will wreak havoc on your blood sugar). There are a few recipes that utilize bread—the Peanut Butter and Chia Jelly French Toast on page 163 and the Thanksgiving Stuffing Kale and Apricot Breakfast Strata, page 168—but I recommend sourdough or sprouted bread, which are easier on your digestion than regular bread (see page 22), and they're always combined with a substantial amount of healthy fat and protein to keep hormones balanced.

Above all, I've formulated these recipes to be as nourishing as they are delicious.

How to Use This Book

Pick a Partner

While you *can* technically make any of the recipes in this book alone, all of them were designed to serve two people, and, as we discussed earlier, you're far more likely to meet your health and happiness goals if you embark on your new lifestyle with another person. You can use this book with your husband, wife, boyfriend, girlfriend, mom, dad, sister, son, daughter, friend, coworker, roommate, workout buddy—the list goes on and on.

The easiest, of course, is someone you live with. You can divide up the labor whichever way works best for your schedule—maybe one partner handles breakfast, another lunch, and you cook dinners together. I do encourage you to get into the kitchen together

to cook at least a few meals a week. For thousands of years, cooking has been an act of love and caregiving, and is hardwired into our brain as such. The bonding that comes from tasting a tomato sauce together or sneaking an extra bit of mise-en-place carrot shouldn't be overlooked. It's also a great time to chat and catch up, while having something else to do with your hands (so good for us introverted types). It's also much faster—for each recipe, I've offered a note on how to divide the labor when you're both in the kitchen together.

You can also easily be Healthier Together with someone else who lives near you or you otherwise see often. Coworkers often have great success at doing this by switching off cooking and bringing breakfasts, lunches, and dinners to the office (you get to cook half as often and eat twice as much!). Friends who don't work together can designate meeting spots to swap food, perhaps even batch-cooking a few days of meals at a time to lighten the load. I highly recommend occasionally cooking dinner or having a Sunday brunch together. While much longevity and health research focuses on what people eat, several experts now believe that the environment in which you eat the food matters just as much, if not more so. When you eat on the run, a cascade of hormones puts your body into a low-level stressed state; energy is diverted away from your stomach and into other organs your body perceives to be in greater need (this is often why people can't eat much when they're nervous). You don't digest your food as well, and the increased levels of cortisol result in increased belly fat, regardless of caloric intake. When you eat with friends, laughing and talking, you're signaling your mind and body that you're in a state of rest. It's biologically healthier, more satisfying, and, frankly, a lot more fun.

Finally, you could also be Healthier Together with people in places far away from you. One of my good friends, who lives in Brooklyn, followed many of the recipes in this book with her mom in California. They each cooked half as often, since the two resulting servings would last each of them for two days. They set up dates using FaceTime, and texted each other photos of their finished dishes to compare. Both mother and daughter came away from the experience galvanized about how easy cooking healthy food could be—and with a deeper appreciation for their relationship. "We ended up talking about what we ate during my childhood, and during hers," my friend said. "I talked to her ten times as much as I normally would."

Dive In

There are a few ways to use this book. The easiest is simply to replace a less than Healthier Together option with a Healthier Together meal. I've arranged the chapters of this book according to the times you'd typically eat with another person, both in and out of your kitchen—at brunch, during happy hour, at a fancy restaurant during date night, or going out for ice cream— offering healthier, homemade alternatives for each one. For the nights you'd just order takeout, I offer remade versions of the classics; and for the times you just need food, the Fast, Cheap, and Easy section gets dinner on the table in less than 20 minutes, using super-simple ingredients that you likely already have on hand.

You can also make the meals on your own, simply packing up the second serving as the kind of leftovers you'll actually look forward to eating (and in just the right amount: my number-one problem with batch-cooking is that by Thursday, I never want to see a bowl of that god-forsaken lentil soup again).

If you'd like to do a bit more of an overhaul, I recommend starting with the Healthier Together 21-Day Cleanup (page 231). According to habit expert Gretchen Rubin, it actually takes far longer than the oft-quoted 21 days to form a habit, but I still find three weeks to be a nice chunk of time to tweak patterns, especially when it comes to healthy eating. It's long enough for you to really start to feel the positive effects of eating healthy—you should begin to have more energy, sleep better, have fewer mood swings and more glowing skin, and, yes, maybe even find a more comfortably happy weight.

What You Need

Equipment

The good news is you don't need a ton of fancy tools to get Healthier Together. You do need a kitchen with an oven and stovetop (hey, I live in New York City—you really never know).

You need standard-size **pots** and **pans**, **rimmed baking sheets**, and, for just a few recipes, a 9 × 5-inch **loaf pan**.

A **food processor** and **blender** are recommended and sometimes necessary (although I give other options whenever possible) for several of the recipes. These are two of the workhorses in my kitchen and I recommend investing in high-quality ones if you can (they'll last forever). I like the Cuisinart 8- and 10-cup-capacity food processors. Like many people in the wellness world, I'm obsessed with my Vitamix— but for good reason. A green smoothie or soup blended in a Vitamix will be silky and completely smooth. If you don't want to splurge on a Vitamix, the NutriBullet is a great alternative. The container is a bit smaller, so you might have to blend in batches for soups or larger dishes, but it's a good deal.

I also recommend investing in a good 8-inch **chef's knife**. The Misono UX10 Gyutou 8.2" is my knife of choice, but many work well. A sharp chef's knife makes prepping infinitely easier and safer—you're actually far more likely to hurt yourself forcing a dull knife through a vegetable than sliding smoothly through with a sharper one.

Ingredients

While I took pains in writing these recipes to include ingredients you can find in almost every grocery store, I do call for a few that may be a bit unfamiliar—but once you get to know them, I promise you'll love them, too! I also have some notes here on what I mean when I call for some more familiar ingredients.

While vegetable or grapeseed oil is often the fat of choice in restaurants and cookbooks—it's cheap and has a neutral flavor that doesn't get in the way of the food—it's also high in omega-6s, which have been shown to cause inflammation in the body, leading to discomfort and disease. These are the oils I recommend cooking with instead, all of which are good high-heat oils, which means they don't oxidize at higher cooking temperatures. Throughout the book, I'll recommend which of these four types of cooking oils I prefer for each recipe or indicate when they can be used interchangeably. If I just specify one type of oil, try to stick to that, since it likely matters for the flavor or texture of the finished dish. If I just say "high-heat oil" with no specification as to which one to use in that recipe, use whichever of the four you have on hand.

Avocado oil is simply the oil pressed from the pulp of avocado, and, as such, contains many of the same benefits as the avocado itself. About 70 percent of avocado oil is heart-healthy oleic acid, a monounsaturated omega-9 fatty acid. Its biggest benefit culinarily is its very neutral, vegetable oil–like flavor and that, unlike ghee and coconut oil, it's liquid at room temperature, which makes it great for baked goods that require liquid fat, and for rubbing on colder ingredients easily (like before roasting vegetables).

Coconut oil is a healthy cooking option, though I don't think it's the miracle ingredient many people in the wellness community give it credit for. It contains lauric acid, which gives it antibacterial, antiviral, and antifungal properties, and studies have shown that regular consumption of coconut oil actually helps people lose belly fat. That said, I wouldn't go stirring it into my coffee. I think it's always better to get fat in whole form (nuts, avocados, etc.), reserving oils for cooking and baking. Coconut oil has a mild, slightly sweet flavor and a high smoke point, making it great for stir-fries. Always look for the unrefined version, which is less processed and preserves more of its health benefits.

Ghee is a type of clarified butter made from simmering butter and skimming off the milk solids that rise to the surface. It's safe for people who can't tolerate lactose, and, unlike dairy, it doesn't contribute to acne. It's a rich source of vitamins A, D, and E, which benefit the skin, hormones, and just about every system in the body (in winter months, I like to include even more of it in my diet, to supplement the lack of sunlight). It tastes like a richer butter, but has a higher smoke point and is less likely to burn. Always look for ghee from grass-fed or pastured cows. I like the brands Ancient Organics and Fourth & Heart.

Let's Talk about Fat

If you haven't yet heard the news, fat doesn't make you fat. The original myth seems to have been started by the sugar lobby, since low-fat foods tend to have tons of added sugar to make them taste, well, edible. I always advise against consuming low-fat foods, simply because I believe that whole foods are better—if you're taking something out, you're modifying it and skewing the perfected balance present in nature.

In general, I don't think fat is something to be feared, but I don't think people should be heaping tons of extra fat in the form of oil into their diet, either. Fat is necessary for the absorption of many vitamins, particularly those found in vegetables (if you're eating a salad or drinking a green smoothie without fat, you're missing out on vitamins A, D, K, and E, which kind of defeats the purpose, doesn't it?). Fat is also necessary for hormone health, brain health, glowing skin, and more. *Healthier Together* recipes embrace fat, but in reasonable amounts and in whole food forms.

Olive oil used to be recommended only in raw form by the health food community, who cited its low smoke point. I've always questioned this though (Italians have been cooking with it for centuries!), and recent research points to it actually being one of the healthiest cooking oils, even at high temperatures. It's rich in longevity-promoting polyphenols and has a grassy, fresh flavor. Just make sure you're using real, high-quality extra virgin olive oil—I like Lucini, which is reasonably priced and widely available.

Nutritional yeast is one of those vegan replacement ingredients I shied away from for a long time. The small flakes (they look kind of like fish food) are made by culturing then deactivating yeast. It's a rich source of complete protein and B vitamins, both of which are often lacking in vegan diets, but the reason I love it is its robust cheesy flavor. Once I got on board the nutritional yeast train (it started with popcorn I received at the office and, oh my God, was it addictive!), I was fully on board. Sometimes, it lends a cheesier flavor than real cheese (try the Honeyed Chive and Cheddar Biscuits on page 49 to taste for yourself) and its texture makes it uniquely good for flavoring popcorn (see Cheesy Turmeric Rosemary Popcorn, page 129).

Arrowroot powder is a starch sourced from tubers. Its big advantage over cornstarch is that it doesn't rely on harsh chemicals for its extraction—rather, it can simply be dried and ground. Arrowroot has been found in studies to help with digestion, treat urinary tract infections, and boost immunity. I like it, though, for its culinary properties. I use it to thicken my Blackberry Ketchup (page 132), and to dry and add starch to the accompanying Carrot Fries so they turn out really crispy.

Hemp seeds, also called hulled hemp hearts, are the seed of the hemp plant (before you ask: no, they don't contain THC and, no, they can't get you high). They're a great source of complete protein and offer a creamy texture with no cream necessary (this is why they pop up in the Fully Loaded Baked Potato-less Soup on page 66). Because they blend up so easily, you can also use them to make a quick nondairy milk in a pinch; just blend a few tablespoons of them with water, and use the resulting milk in your Peanut Butter and Chia Jelly French Toast (page 163) or morning coffee for an extra hit of protein. Because hemp is a bio-accumulator (it's planted to clean up soil after radiation incidents), it's super-important to buy organic whenever possible. Store your hemp seeds in the fridge or freezer to protect their nutrients and prevent them from getting rancid.

Chia seeds perform a magic trick when they get wet, turning thick and gelatinous. The resulting gel can be used like an egg, to bind things like Carrot Cake Breakfast Cookies (page 172), or to add viscosity, as in the Honey-Rose Rice Pudding (page 228). Aztec warriors used to eat chia seeds for an energy boost, and they're high in antioxidants that keep skin looking youthful and supple. They're also an amazing digestive aid—top doctor and best-selling author Terry Wahls, MD, who is famous for healing her multiple sclerosis, cites them as her favorite constipation-reducing, gut-healing food.

Salt Unless stated otherwise, when I call for salt, I mean fine-grain sea salt. Sea salt has all its minerals intact, which I like because minerals are great, and, in general (you'll notice a theme here), I prefer ingredients in their most natural state. A good way to tell if your salt is unrefined is if it has some color to it—real salt is almost never pure white. Sea salt comes in coarse and flaky forms, but I find that the fine-grain stuff becomes better incorporated when cooking. I love Redmond Real Salt, Celtic Sea Salt, and pink Himalayan. If you use a different kind, use it sparingly and taste your food often, since different salts have varying levels of salinity.

I also call for flaky Maldon salt, for finishing. This is another type of sea salt, but with much larger crystals, which provide a delicious, salty crunch on top of baked goods, but don't incorporate well when used in normal cooking.

Spices I use spices liberally throughout this book, both for their potent flavor and their health benefits—I think of them as the original superfoods. They're gut-healing, calming, anti-inflammatory, metabolism-boosting, and more. However, if you get irradiated spices (which most supermarket brands are), they're exposed to ionizing radiation before being bottled, which significantly reduces their healthful properties. Lower-quality spices also tend to be less flavorful—potent flavor, in fact, is a great indicator of potent health benefits. The two brands I favor for their high-quality sourcing, freshness, and potency are Simply Organic and Frontier Co-Op.

Collagen, or hydrolyzed collagen, has become a bit of a trendy ingredient in recent years, but I think this one has staying power. Made from the connective tissues of either fish or cows, it's the most abundant protein in the human body, which uses it to grow hair, skin, and nails. A number of studies have shown its ability to improve skin elasticity and make hair and nails grow faster and stronger, but perhaps more exciting is its ability to help "seal" the gut lining and help prevent gut inflammation. Having a healthy gut is key for a healthy brain, immune system, and more, so this property is incredibly exciting. It's also been found to alleviate joint pain, and is high in protein, making it a good whole-food protein supplement. It doesn't really have a flavor, and dissolves readily in hot or cold liquids. Finally, consuming collagen helps trigger the release of sleep-inducing melatonin in your body, which is why it's the perfect inclusion in Raspberry White Chocolate Moon Milk (page 227). Always look for grass-fed sources of collagen, which is third-party tested to ensure that it's free of contaminants and heavy metals. I like Vital Proteins and Great Lakes.

Gelatin is very similar to collagen, but it hasn't been processed to break down its proteins and thus reacts differently when combined with a liquid. Its health benefits are the same as collagen's, but when treated properly in liquid, it'll form a gel, making it the perfect base for gut-healing Cinnamon Vanilla Bean Marshmallows (page 220). You can also spoon some into hot tea—the tea will become slightly more viscous and much more gut healing. Never sub collagen for gelatin or vice versa, as you'll get completely different results. Vital Proteins and Great Lakes both make great gelatin.

Soy sauce/tamari While many people use tamari and soy sauce interchangeably, there are a few key differences. Because tamari is made from a by-product of miso (a gut-healing fermented paste that adds umami to dishes like the Kombucha-Miso Massaged Kale Salad on page 119), instead of a ferment made from soybeans and wheat, like soy sauce, it's generally gluten-free (but always check the label if you have celiac disease, since a few brands add wheat to the ferment). Tamari has a smoother, richer, more consistently salty flavor than soy sauce and contains niacin (vitamin B_3), manganese, and tryptophan, a natural mood enhancer. It's far less likely to contain additives or artificial colorants, and has about 30 percent more protein. If you only have soy sauce on hand, it's a fine substitute, but next time you need a restock, consider tamari as an alternative.

Nondairy milk I don't cook with dairy milk—I've seen enough science and heard personal stories about how it causes mucus, acne, and inflammation to form in the body to want to steer clear. These days, there are a ton of nondairy milks available that work as wonderful substitutes. I prefer the kinds found in the refrigerated section of the grocery store, and always, *always* check the ingredients list for added sugars, emulsifiers, and stabilizers like carrageenan, which can wreak havoc in your gut. So Delicious and Califia Farms both make great versions.

You can also easily make your own nondairy milk and keep a batch in the fridge to use throughout the week.

I also love using canned coconut milk, which adds a creamy texture, sweet taste, and tons of antiviral, antifungal, and antibacterial properties to dishes (always check for BPA-free cans).

Apple cider vinegar is another ingredient that's become something of a health world darling, with some backable claims and others that lean more toward hype. The biggest reason to use apple cider vinegar as opposed to white vinegar or balsamic is that it's often sold unpasteurized, with the "mother" intact. You'll see this denoted clearly on the bottle (always look for it) and also inside the vinegar, as a more opaque cloudiness that settles at the bottom of the bottle. This part of the vinegar contains the bulk of its health benefits, and has antioxidant, antibacterial, and antifungal properties. Apple cider vinegar can help settle the stomach and lower blood sugar levels—one study showed that it reduced blood sugar by 34 percent after eating a carb-heavy meal. It's far and away my favorite vinegar to use, for both its health benefits and mildly sweet-and-sour taste— just be sure not to heat it, as that eliminates many of its benefits. Combined with nondairy

milk, it also makes a perfect substitute for buttermilk, which you'll see utilized in Cornflake "Fried" Chicken (page 97) and the super-fluffy Cardamom Banana-Bread Pancakes (page 154).

Flour I rely on whole-plant flours, like almond, coconut, oat, and chickpea, for a few reasons. They're naturally gluten-free, and generally are less inflammatory and irritating to the gut than white or whole-wheat flour. They're also a whole food—you could theoretically make all the flours used in this book by yourself in a blender, meaning you're not missing out on any synergistic nutrients. Finally, because they're rich in protein, healthy fat, and fiber, they keep your blood sugar level stable and won't wreak havoc on your hormones—unlike white bread and flour, which have actually been found in studies to spike your blood sugar more than white sugar!

Bread While I don't use processed flours, I am okay with small amounts of bread, if it's properly prepared. Until about 100 years ago, all grains were fermented or sprouted before being consumed, undergoing this time-intensive process (often 72 hours or more) to make the grains more digestible and less irritating. Because you're unlikely to do this at home, I don't include grains in the book; luckily, you can now find bakeries and brands willing to ferment or sprout grains for you; hence the small amount of allowed bread. I like to buy sourdough at a local bakery (bonus points if it's made with ancient grains—think bulgur, farro, einkorn, and others). Studies have found that people with gluten sensitivity can digest well-fermented sourdough with

ease. I also like Ezekiel bread, which is sprouted, another activating process that helps grains become less harmful and more bio-available. Of course, if you have celiac disease, go for a gluten-free option.

Eggs are a protein-rich cornerstone of a healthy diet, great for hormone health and rich in vital nutrients, like choline, selenium, vitamin B_{12}, and vitamin A. Reach for pastured or pasture-raised eggs, which means eggs from chickens that are allowed to roam freely, consuming a large variety of foods, including bugs and grubs. Confusingly, pastured eggs will almost never be certified organic, since the farmer would have to have organic certification for the entire area the chicken roams. It's also not a regulated term—many brands will claim their eggs are pastured, while noting in smaller letters that their chickens are "fed a vegetarian diet." I prefer to buy eggs from a local farmer's market whenever possible, but Vital Farms is my favorite pick from a grocery store. If you can't find pasture-raised, organic is the next best option. "Free-range," an unregulated term, means almost nothing. Like most unadulterated food, pasture-raised eggs tend to be on the smaller side, and don't typically come in the "jumbo" variety, so if you use larger eggs, adjust the recipes accordingly.

Fast, Cheap & Easy

This chapter could also be called "No Excuses," as it's designed to save you from grabbing whatever unhealthy food is closest when you're tired or in a hurry. Every recipe here can be made in less than 20 minutes, and they mostly rely on pantry staples (no fancy or out-there ingredients here). Use it to hold your Healthier Together partner accountable, too—if they're having an "I just can't cook tonight" moment, remind them that you're mere minutes from a plateful of satay-covered Thai salad or the best pesto pasta you've ever had.

TIP: You can use infused milk or water when making any grains, sweet or savory. Simply steep any herb or tea in the just-boiled liquid for about 10 minutes, covered, like you're making tea, then proceed as desired. I love using basil, lavender, green tea, herbal teas, and citrus peels.

Pumpkin & Rosemary Savory Porridge with Sautéed Mushrooms

Serves 2

1½ cups nondairy milk

2 sprigs fresh rosemary, plus more for garnish, if desired

1 cup canned pumpkin purée

¼ teaspoon fine-grain sea salt

1 cup rolled oats

3 tablespoons avocado oil or ghee

½ pound mushrooms, sliced (I like shiitake and button)

2 teaspoons apple cider vinegar

2 teaspoons tamari

1 garlic clove, minced

2 tablespoons pomegranate seeds, for garnish (optional)

I've always found it a shame that oatmeal is confined to breakfast when its health benefits and easy prep beat out many of the more common dinners. Here an oat base takes on a distinctively savory (and, dare I say, sophisticated?) profile. It's cooked in rosemary-infused milk, which imparts a subtle woodiness, then swirled with fiber and vitamin A–packed pumpkin purée. Mushrooms add a satisfying, umami chew that brings the dish decidedly into the dinner zone, while pomegranate seeds add a sweet crunch (and, let's be real, they're also super-pretty, but feel free to skip them). If you're cooking this with your partner, have one of you make the oats while the other tackles the mushrooms.

1. **Make the oatmeal:** Bring the milk to a boil in a small pot over medium heat. Remove the pot from the heat, add the rosemary, and cover. Let the mixture steep for 10 minutes, then remove and discard the rosemary sprigs (it's okay if a few leaves fall loose).

2. Stir in the pumpkin purée and salt until smooth, then return to a boil over medium-high heat. Add the oats and reduce the heat to medium. Simmer uncovered until the oats are mostly thickened and cooked through, about 5 minutes. Remove the porridge from the heat.

3. **Meanwhile, make the mushrooms:** Heat the oil in a medium skillet over medium heat. When it shimmers, add the mushrooms and cook for 3 to 4 minutes, until they begin to soften and brown. Reduce the heat to medium-low and add the apple cider vinegar, tamari, and garlic. Sauté until the mushrooms are tender, about 8 more minutes.

4. Divide the oatmeal between 2 bowls. Top with the mushrooms and garnish with the pomegranate seeds, if using, and a sprig of rosemary, if desired.

Round-the-World Avocado Egg Boats

Serves 2

FOR THE EGG BOATS

2 ripe avocados, halved and pitted

4 medium eggs

¼ teaspoon fine-grain sea salt

When I sent an email out to all the doctors I work with (most of whom are bestselling authors, all of whom are among the country's absolute best), asking what they thought was the number-one healthiest food, the vast majority of them said avocado. "They are delicious, nutritious, and full of healthy fats that help keep us feeling satiated and nourished," explains Dr. Frank Lipman. "They contain over twenty different vitamins and minerals, antioxidants, and are a great source of fiber." Here I crack an egg for protein and top it with satisfying, crunchy seasoning to make it a meal. If you're making this with a partner, have one of you handle the egg-in-avocado task, and the other whip up one of the topping options.

1. Preheat the oven to 350°F.

2. Make the avocado egg boats: Place the avocados, cut side up, in a small baking dish (there should be enough room for them to be in a single layer without touching each other). Carefully crack the eggs, separating the yolks and whites into separate small bowls. Using a spoon, transfer one yolk into each avocado half. Beat the fine-grain sea salt into the egg whites, then spoon it into the avocado halves, without spilling over. Bake until the whites are set and the yolks are slightly runny, about 20 minutes.

3. Meanwhile, in a small mixing bowl, mix together your seasoning blend of choice (for the furikake blend, don't mix in the tamari or sriracha; simply dash them onto the finished avocado). Top the finished avocados liberally with your mix of choice before dividing between 2 plates and serving immediately.

Topping Options

EVERYTHING BAGEL SEASONING

1 tablespoon coarse sea salt

1 tablespoon white sesame seeds

1 tablespoon dried onion flakes

1 tablespoon poppy seeds

1 tablespoon dried garlic flakes

1 tablespoon caraway seeds

ROSY HARISSA

2 teaspoons chili powder

½ teaspoon ground coriander

½ teaspoon ground cumin

½ teaspoon caraway seeds

1 teaspoon crushed culinary rose petals

½ teaspoon dried mint leaves

CHEESY THYME

2 tablespoons nutritional yeast

1 tablespoon fresh thyme, minced

8 toasted almonds, crushed or finely chopped

Maldon salt, for sprinkling

FURIKAKE

1 sheet toasted nori seaweed, crumbled

1 tablespoon toasted white sesame seeds

1 tablespoon toasted black sesame seeds

Maldon salt, for sprinkling

Dash of tamari or soy sauce

Dash of sriracha

Frozen Broccoli & Basil Soup with Sweet and Spicy Cashews

Serves 2

FOR THE SOUP

1 tablespoon high-heat oil

1 medium yellow onion, chopped

3 cups frozen or fresh broccoli florets

½ teaspoon fine-grain sea salt, plus more to taste

1 cup packed fresh basil leaves

1 (13.5-ounce) can coconut milk (either full-fat or reduced-fat works fine)

Juice of 1 lime

FOR THE CASHEWS

⅓ cup raw cashews, chopped

2 tablespoons honey

¼ teaspoon paprika

¼ teaspoon fine-grain sea salt

I'm always frustrated with how infrequently cookbooks call for frozen ingredients, especially given what nutrient powerhouses they can be—not to mention their convenience. Frozen broccoli doesn't sit on trucks or the shelf losing nutrients for weeks on end, so it's likely to be *more* nutrient-dense than its fresh counterpart—and often more cost-effective, and likely to be readily accessible (I don't know about you, but my fresh broccoli often gets lost in my fridge before dying a mushy death). Of course, this recipe works with the fresh stuff, if you have it on hand. With just a few other pantry staples, broccoli turns into a herbaceous soup, brought to life with sweet and spicy cashews for a satisfying crunch in every bite. If you're making this with a partner, have one of you handle the cashews and the other whip up the soup.

1. **Make the soup:** Heat the oil in a medium pot over medium-high heat. When it shimmers, add the onions and cook, stirring occasionally, until translucent, about 5 minutes. Reduce the heat to medium, and stir in the broccoli, ½ cup water, and the sea salt. Cover and cook until the broccoli is bright green and tender, about 5 minutes. Transfer half the mixture to a blender with the basil, coconut milk, and lime juice. Blend until very smooth, then add the remaining half of the mixture and pulse until it is mostly smooth, with a bit of desired texture. (You could also use an immersion blender to do this right in the pot; just remove half the mixture first, then add it back.) Return to the pot and rewarm to the desired temperature. Sprinkle with additional salt to taste.

2. Meanwhile, **make the honey-chili cashews:** Place the cashews in a small, dry skillet over medium heat. Cook until the cashews begin to turn golden, about 5 minutes. Add the honey, paprika, and salt, and stir until the cashews are well-coated. Remove the pan from the heat.

3. Divide the soup between 2 bowls, and top each with half the nut mixture (it'll be a generous portion—you want cashews in every bite!).

Fresh Tomato & Strawberry Bruschetta

Serves 2

3 tablespoons olive oil

2 green onions, white and light green parts only, chopped

½ teaspoon fine-grain sea salt

2 cups frozen peas, thawed

½ cup fresh mint leaves

3 tablespoons raw, hulled sunflower seeds

1 cup strawberries, hulled and sliced

1 cup cherry tomatoes, halved

Freshly ground black pepper

4 slices sourdough bread or healthy bread of choice (see page 22)

1 lemon

Maldon salt, for sprinkling

I'm not sure when we decided that things between two slices of bread—that is, sandwiches—constituted a meal and an open-faced bruschetta was relegated to the appetizer realm, especially since the toppings are the tastiest (and healthiest!) part. I especially love this toast during spring and summer, when the cherry tomatoes and strawberries are bursting with flavor (peas are in season around the same time, but I refuse to make you shuck them for a modicum of flavor improvement). Don't skip the Maldon salt. A staple among chefs everywhere, it elevates almost every dish, with pops of crunch and salinity. If you're making this with a partner, have one of you prepare the peas while the other pan-roasts the sunflower seeds and tosses the tomato-strawberry topping.

1. In a small pot, combine 2 tablespoons of olive oil, the green onions, ¼ teaspoon of fine-grain sea salt, and the peas. Cover and cook over medium-low heat for 2 to 4 minutes, until the peas are bright green. Transfer to a food processor. Add the mint leaves and pulse until very smooth. (If you don't have a food processor, you can mash with a fork; just finely chop the mint first.)

2. Meanwhile, place the sunflower seeds in a small, dry skillet. Toast over medium-low heat, stirring occasionally, until golden, 3 to 5 minutes.

3. In a medium bowl, gently toss the strawberries and tomatoes with the remaining 1 tablespoon of olive oil, ¼ teaspoon of fine-grain sea salt, and a generous amount of freshly ground pepper until combined.

4. Spread the mashed peas on the toast. Top with the strawberry-tomato mixture. Add a squeeze of fresh lemon, the sunflower seeds, and a generous sprinkle of Maldon salt. Serve immediately.

Red Pepper, Sausage & Onion Stir-Fry with Toasty Fennel Seeds

Serves 2

1 tablespoon fennel seeds

1 tablespoon avocado oil

1 red bell pepper, seeded and sliced

½ medium (or 1 small) yellow onion, sliced

½ teaspoon fine-grain sea salt

1 large bunch Swiss chard or other hearty greens, stems removed and leaves roughly torn into bite-size pieces, 5 to 6 loosely packed cups

2 precooked Italian-flavored sausages (I like the organic Aidell's and Teton Waters Ranch), sliced into bite-size pieces

2 garlic cloves, minced

This dish tastes just like sausage and onion pizza, except it's naturally gluten-free and takes just minutes to make. The layers of savory flavor keep on multiplying, and the fennel seeds add an extra Italian crunch, plus tons of stomach-soothing benefits. No need to be picky about the greens here—any hearty green works well (think collards, kale, mustard greens). If you want to make the dish vegetarian, simply substitute one can of drained, rinsed white beans for the sausage, and proceed with the recipe as usual.

1. Place the fennel seeds in a large skillet over medium heat. Toast, shaking the pan occasionally, until fragrant and just beginning to turn golden, 3 to 4 minutes. Remove from the heat and use a mortar and pestle or the bottom of a sturdy jar on a plate to crush the fennel seeds. Set aside.

2. Return the pan to medium heat and add the avocado oil. When it shimmers, add the red pepper, onions, and ¼ teaspoon of salt, and cook, stirring occasionally, until golden brown and reduced in volume by half, about 15 minutes.

3. Add the greens, sausage, and the remaining ¼ teaspoon of salt, tossing to coat the greens with the oil. Cook until the greens have wilted and the sausage is beginning to brown, about 5 minutes, stirring occasionally. Stir in the garlic and cook for 2 more minutes.

4. Divide the stir-fry between 2 bowls or plates, and top with the crunchy crushed fennel seeds. Serve immediately.

Our Go-To Chilaquiles

Serves 2

4 (6-inch) corn tortillas, cut into 8 triangles each (like pizza slices)

4 teaspoons avocado oil

¾ teaspoon fine-grain sea salt

4 medium eggs

1 teaspoon chili powder

1 teaspoon ground cumin

½ teaspoon garlic powder

½ teaspoon onion powder

¼ teaspoon smoked paprika

1 small yellow onion, chopped

1 (15-ounce) can black beans, drained and rinsed

⅓ cup salsa

1 lime, cut in half

2 green onions, white and light green parts only, sliced

¼ cup chopped fresh cilantro

TIP: If you don't want to turn the oven on, you can use pre-made tortilla chips (although it will be less healthful, as the ones here are baked, not fried). Just look for an organic version since most corn is GMO and heavily sprayed, and thick-cut chips so they don't turn to mush.

Chilaquiles have always been my go-to hangover breakfast of choice. They have just the right amount of carbs to sop up my booze belly, plus plenty of protein from the black beans and eggs to be super-satiating. Eventually, Zack and I started making them for dinner, too—they're just that good. This is our favorite recipe; it relies on dried spices to make a pseudo-taco seasoning that elevates the flavor and cuts way down on the prep time. Cooking the eggs over low heat gives them a creamy texture that mimics the addition of cheese, but with no dairy necessary. Think of it as a ten-minute Mexican casserole, with all the comfort and none of the stomachaches.

1. Preheat the oven to 400°F. On a large baking sheet lined with parchment paper, toss the corn tortilla triangles with 2 teaspoons of the oil and ½ teaspoon of the salt. Bake until golden brown and crispy, 8 to 10 minutes, flipping the tortillas and rotating the pan halfway through.

2. Meanwhile, in a medium bowl, beat together the eggs, chili powder, cumin, garlic powder, onion powder, smoked paprika, and remaining ¼ teaspoon salt until very smooth.

3. Heat the remaining 2 teaspoons of oil in a large skillet over medium-high heat. Add the onions and cook, stirring occasionally, until they begin to brown, about 3 minutes. Reduce heat to low, then add the black beans and cook until the beans are warmed through and the onions are translucent, about 8 minutes.

4. Add the cooked tortilla chips and the egg mixture, stirring to coat the chips with the egg, and cook, stirring constantly, until the eggs are set, 1 to 2 minutes. Add the salsa and stir to coat the tortilla mixture evenly, before removing the skillet from the heat. Divide between two plates and top each with the juice from half a lime, and half of the green onions and chopped cilantro. Serve immediately.

10-Minute Poke Bowl

Serves 2

FOR THE DRESSING

2 tablespoons tamari or soy sauce

1 tablespoon white miso paste

2 garlic cloves, minced

½ teaspoon rice vinegar

¼ teaspoon ground ginger

½ teaspoon sesame seeds

¾ teaspoon toasted sesame oil

FOR THE POKE

½ pound sushi-grade ahi tuna (see "What's the Deal with Buying Fish," page 183), cut into ½-inch cubes, or 2 golden or red beets, cut into ½-inch cubes, boiled, and chilled

FOR SERVING (OPTIONAL)

2 cups cooked white rice or quinoa

2 cups mixed greens

1 cup thinly sliced purple cabbage

1 avocado, peeled, pitted, and cubed

4 green onions, white and light green parts only, thinly sliced

2 tablespoons pickled ginger

½ cup roughly chopped fresh cilantro

2 teaspoons red pepper flakes

1 teaspoon furikake

Poke bowls are one of those mysterious foods that people think they can never replicate at home, when, really, they're one of the easier dishes out there. In fact, they're commonly served at convenience stores and gas stations in Hawaii! Here you can choose to make a traditional poke bowl with tuna, swap in beets for the fish, or (my preference!) go half and half. The dressing and toppings are really what take it to the next level: miso injects a delicate funk with gut-healing probiotics, while the tamari umamis it up. Go crazy with the toppings—they all add nutritional benefits, and make the result more pleasing to the palate and eye. If you're making this dish with your partner, put one of you on toppings duty and have the other handle the dressing and main dish.

1. **Make the dressing:** In a large bowl, whisk together the tamari, white miso paste, minced garlic cloves, rice vinegar, ground ginger, sesame seeds, and toasted sesame oil.

2. **Make the poke:** Add the tuna and/or beets to the dressing and toss to coat. Marinate for 10 minutes. Serve the poke over your base of choice, topped as you'd like.

Chopped Thai Satay Salad

Serves 2

FOR THE SALAD

½ cup raw, unsalted peanuts or nuts of choice

2 carrots, trimmed and roughly chopped

3 green onions, white and light green parts only, roughly chopped

1 red bell pepper, seeded and roughly chopped

½ head purple cabbage, roughly chopped

1 cup fresh cilantro, roughly chopped

FOR THE DRESSING

¼ cup peanut butter or nut butter of choice

Juice of 1 lime

2 garlic cloves, minced or grated

2 teaspoons peeled, minced ginger

2 tablespoons tamari or soy sauce

1 tablespoon toasted sesame oil

1 tablespoon maple syrup

Generous pinch of cayenne pepper (optional)

Thai satay's genius is that it takes boring, bland chicken and makes it completely drool-worthy, using a perfectly spiced, just-sweet-enough-just-savory-enough peanut sauce. Here I've taken that sauce and poured it over a bowl of rainbow vegetables, making for a far more beautiful and flavorful finished product. I like to use a food processor to make this dish extra easy, but if you don't have one, just roughly chop all the vegetables—don't worry about being precise. Feel free to sub in whatever veggies you like, or switch up the nuts and nut butter. If you're making it with a partner, put one of you in charge of chopping or processing while the other whips up the dressing.

1. **Make the salad:** Preheat the oven to 350°F. Line a baking sheet with parchment paper and spread out the peanuts in a single layer. Toast until golden brown, about 5 minutes. Remove and let cool.

2. Place the carrots in a food processor fitted with the shredding disk. Pulse a few times until rough-chopped but not riced. Transfer to a large bowl and repeat with the green onions, red bell pepper, purple cabbage, and peanuts, working one at a time with each ingredient. (If you do them at the same time, they process unevenly and you'll get some riced vegetables and some huge chunks.)

3. **Make the dressing:** In a medium bowl, whisk together the peanut butter, lime juice, garlic, ginger, tamari, toasted sesame oil, maple syrup, and cayenne (if using).

4. Pour the dressing over the vegetables and toss to coat well. Mix in the cilantro and divide between 2 plates. Serve immediately.

Mint & Cilantro Pesto Pasta with Lemon-Pistachio Crumbs

Serves 2

½ teaspoon plus ⅛ teaspoon fine-grain sea salt, plus more for the pasta water

2 cups dried pasta of choice

1 cup raw, shelled pistachios

Grated zest and juice of 1 lemon

½ cup olive oil

1 cup packed fresh cilantro

1 cup packed fresh mint leaves

4 garlic cloves

1 tablespoon raw honey

TIP: There are a ton of great alternatives to refined wheat pasta brands out there (Trader Joe's makes a great red lentil blend, and the ancient grain–based TruRoots blends are awesome), but you can also toss the pesto with spiralized zucchini or sweet potato noodles if you're looking for an even more veg-heavy dinner.

Whenever I make pasta, I double the typical amount of sauce to increase my vegetable-to-carb ratio. This pesto is a great way to eat several servings of greens without even realizing you're doing it, and the pistachios add a meatiness (and a helping of hormone-stabilizing protein and fat!) that makes this dish feel like a hearty meal. This version uses detoxifying cilantro and stomach-soothing mint for a zesty, distinctive flavor, but feel free to sub in whichever herbs or greens you have on hand (basil, spinach, parsley . . .); the combination of garlic, lemon, and honey pairs well with anything.

1. Bring a large pot of water to a boil over high heat. Add a small palmful of salt. Add the pasta and cook according to package instructions until al dente. Drain and return to the pot off the heat.

2. Meanwhile, place the pistachios in a medium skillet over low heat. Toast, tossing occasionally, until fragrant and just beginning to turn golden brown, about 3 minutes. Transfer ¼ cup of the pistachios to a food processor. Add the lemon zest and ⅛ teaspoon of salt and pulse until it's the size of pebbles. Transfer to a small bowl.

3. Without wiping out the food processor, add the olive oil, herbs, remaining ¾ cup of pistachios, lemon juice, garlic, honey, and ½ teaspoon salt. Process until a smooth sauce forms.

4. Pour the pesto over the cooked pasta and toss until the pasta is well coated (there will be a lot of sauce, but it's the healthiest part of the dish, so be generous). Divide between 2 bowls and top with the lemon-pistachio crumbs. Serve immediately.

Foods
You
Crave

You know when you're really committed to eating healthfully, but then someone at work mentions nachos and suddenly all you can think about is gooey, finger-licking cheese and salty tortilla chips. And then, even though you *have* a salad for lunch, you can't actually bring yourself to eat the damn thing? This chapter is for those moments. Filled with hearty foods that will make you drool, it's all somehow still super-healthy. Biscuits and gravy! Latkes! Bolognese! All of 'em are free of inflammatory ingredients, and packed with vegetables. Grab your partner and indulge in the fact that being Healthier Together does *not* mean having less fun. P.S.: The nachos are on page 73. You're welcome.

Enchilada Lasagna with Avocado Béchamel & Crispy Tortilla Crumble

Serves 2

4 cups (¾-inch cubes) butternut squash

2 tablespoons plus 1 teaspoon avocado oil

¾ teaspoon chipotle powder

½ teaspoon dried oregano

1¼ teaspoons fine-grain sea salt

1 lime

1 cup raw cashews, soaked 2–6 hours and drained

1 large ripe avocado, peeled and pitted

12 (6-inch) corn tortillas

1 (15-ounce) can black beans, drained and rinsed

2½ cups tomatillo salsa

3 garlic cloves

¼ cup packed fresh cilantro

Enchiladas and lasagna are two of the ultimate comfort foods, and this dish incorporates the best of both; a bright-green, super-fresh Mexican lasagna somehow meets every expectation you have. The avocado béchamel is a creamy wonder, and the crispy tortilla crumble on top adds a salty crunch that will make you forget cheese ever existed (well, not really, but it's damn good). While tomatillo salsa is widely available (you can find it at Trader Joe's, most grocery stores, and online—it's the only green salsa), you can also make your own if you'd like—follow the instructions in the Tip on page 48. Also, because corn is a widely sprayed crop, look for organic tortillas whenever possible.

1. Preheat the oven to 450°F.

2. Arrange the butternut squash on a parchment paper–lined baking sheet in a single layer. Add 1 tablespoon of avocado oil, the chipotle powder, dried oregano, and ½ teaspoon of salt, and toss to coat. Bake for 30 to 40 minutes, flipping halfway through, until the edges are brown and the squash is tender. Remove the squash from the oven and reduce the oven temperature to 375°F.

3. Zest the lime onto a plate or into a small bowl and set aside.

4. Meanwhile, **make the béchamel:** Place the soaked cashews, avocado, and ¼ teaspoon of salt in a food processor. Squeeze in the juice from the lime. Process until very smooth, about 1 minute. Transfer the béchamel to a medium bowl and wipe out the food processor.

(recipe continues)

TIP: If you want to make your own tomatillo salsa, toss 1 head of garlic (broken into cloves) and 1 pound of tomatillos with 2 tablespoons of avocado oil and ¾ teaspoon of fine-grain sea salt. Roast for 10 minutes at 450°F until the tomatillos are brown on the bottom, then flip and roast for 5 more minutes. Let them cool slightly before transferring to a food processor and pulsing with 1 small yellow onion, 1 seeded jalapeño, and ½ cup of packed fresh cilantro.

5. Add 1 teaspoon of avocado oil to a 10-inch cast-iron skillet or pie dish and swirl to coat evenly. Place 3 tortillas in the skillet to cover the bottom. Spread half of the béchamel evenly over the tortillas. Cover the béchamel with half of the butternut squash, half of the black beans, and 1 cup of tomatillo salsa. Turn the skillet slightly and place 3 more tortillas on top, covering any gaps. Add the remaining béchamel, butternut squash, black beans, and another 1 cup of salsa. Turn the skillet, add 3 more tortillas, again covering any gaps, and cover evenly with the remaining ½ cup of salsa. Bake for 30 minutes, or until completely warmed through.

6. While the lasagna bakes, **make the tortilla topping:** Tear the remaining 3 tortillas into chip-size pieces. Toss on a parchment-lined baking sheet with the remaining 1 tablespoon of oil and ½ teaspoon of salt until well-coated. Bake the tortillas with the lasagna until golden and crispy, about 10 minutes. Remove the tortilla chips from the oven and let cool for 5 minutes, then transfer to the food processor. Add the garlic, cilantro, and lime zest, and pulse until pebble-sized, with a few larger pieces of tortilla. Taste and add more salt as needed.

7. Remove the lasagna from the oven and top with the crumbly tortilla mixture. Let cool for 10 minutes before serving.

Honeyed Chive & "Cheddar" Biscuits with Rosemary Cauliflower Gravy

Serves 2

FOR THE GRAVY

1 tablespoon ghee or avocado oil

1 small yellow onion, chopped

½ teaspoon fine-grain sea salt

1 small head of cauliflower, roughly chopped

4 garlic cloves, minced

1 teaspoon chopped fresh rosemary

1 teaspoon chopped fresh thyme

¼ pound cooked pastured chicken or pork breakfast sausage, crumbled (optional)

FOR THE BISCUITS

½ cup oat flour

1 cup almond flour

½ teaspoon fine-grain sea salt

2 teaspoons baking powder

½ teaspoon freshly ground black pepper

⅓ cup finely chopped fresh chives

¼ cup nutritional yeast

2 tablespoons unsalted butter from grass-fed cows or solid coconut oil

2 medium eggs

⅓ cup unsweetened nondairy milk

It sounds impossible to create a perfect, airy biscuit without using inflammatory, hormone-disrupting refined flours, but this recipe nails it. The oat flour adds density, while the almond flour gives a flaky lift. The nutritional yeast lends the biscuits a "cheesier" flavor than actual cheddar cheese (believe it or not!), while also adding a healthful dose of protein and B vitamins. The cauliflower gravy on top is a revelation. This dish might be one of the most soul-satisfying comfort foods around. If you're cooking it with a partner, have one of you make the biscuits while the other preps the gravy.

1. **Make the gravy:** In a large skillet, melt the ghee over medium-low heat. Add the onions, salt, and cauliflower. Cover and cook for 20 to 30 minutes, stirring occasionally, until the cauliflower is very easily pierced with a fork and the mixture is golden brown and jammy. If the cauliflower or onions are sticking to the bottom of pan, add water, ¼ cup at a time, scraping up the brown bits. Add the garlic and sauté for 2 minutes, uncovered, until the garlic is very fragrant and just beginning to turn golden. Transfer roughly three-quarters of the mixture to a blender or food processor. Add 1 cup of water and half of both the rosemary and thyme, and blend until very smooth, about 1 minute.

2. Add the remaining cauliflower mixture, rosemary, thyme, and sausage (if using), and pulse until the gravy is mostly smooth, with a bit of texture remaining and green flecks of rosemary visible.

(recipe continues)

TO SERVE

1 tablespoon honey

Chopped fresh chives, for garnish

Freshly ground black pepper,
for garnish

3. **Make the biscuits:** Preheat the oven to 400°F. Line a baking sheet with parchment paper.

4. In a large bowl, mix the oat flour, almond flour, salt, baking powder, pepper, chives, and nutritional yeast until well combined. Using 2 knives or a pastry cutter, cut the butter into the mixture until it resembles coarse sand. In a medium bowl, beat together 1 egg and the milk. Add the wet mixture to the dry and stir until well combined. Drop the batter by the heaping teaspoonful onto the prepared baking sheet. Beat the second egg in a small bowl and brush liberally over the tops of the biscuits. Bake for 12 to 15 minutes, or until the bottoms are golden brown.

5. **To serve:** Halve the biscuits so they're open-face, spread both halves with honey, and top with a generous ladle-ful of gravy. Sprinkle chives and black pepper on top.

Is Butter a Health Food?

I posed this question to some of the doctors I work with and the reaction was mostly positive. According to Dr. Will Cole, a Pittsburgh-based functional medicine practitioner and author of *Ketotarian*, "Butter is a great source of bio-available, fat-soluble vitamins, like K_2. Our society is greatly deficient in these nutrients, which are essential for supporting hundreds of different pathways that determine our brain, immune, and hormone health. Studies are now showing that saturated fats are not correlated with increased risk of heart disease, as previously thought. Because of mutations of the dairy protein casein, due to years of cross-breeding, it is important to choose ghee (clarified butter) or butter from grass-fed cows, particularly from beta A2 (the original, less inflammatory form of casein) cows."

While the research is pointing toward butter being part of a healthy diet, I still prefer to use it sparingly, typically as a condiment, as in Honey Butter (page 143), or as a baking aid, as in these biscuits or the Chicken Potpie (page 61). For cooking, I prefer to rely on dairy-free ghee, avocado oil, and coconut oil.

Way More Veggies Bolognese

Serves 2

½ teaspoon fine grain sea salt, plus more for the pasta water

2 cups dried pasta of choice

2 tablespoons avocado oil or ghee

¼ pound ground beef

1 cup diced carrot (from 2 medium carrots)

¾ cup diced celery (from 2 small stalks)

1 cup diced yellow onion (from 1 large onion)

¼ cup tomato paste

1 cup canned crushed tomatoes in their juices

Pinch of nutmeg

½ cup canned full-fat coconut milk

¼ cup red wine (preferably organic)

4 garlic cloves, minced

TIP: You can easily make this Bolognese vegan by omitting the beef and adding ½ cup cooked brown or black lentils to the sauce when you add the crushed tomatoes and coconut milk.

I've made it my life's mission to try every Bolognese sauce I come across. I've had them with beef, with pork, with lentils, with cream and without, with red wine and with white. This version, I think, takes the best bits of all of those. First of all, the healthier part: I've flipped the ratio of meat and veggies, so there's just enough beef to be hearty, while leaving far more room for the carrots, celery, and onions. I add the umami back with caramelized tomato paste and a hit of acid with red wine (and I highly recommend you finish the bottle as an accompaniment to your dinner). If you're making this with a partner, one of you can chop vegetables and make the pasta, while the other does the stovetop work.

1. Bring a large pot of water to a boil over high heat. Add a small palmful of salt. Add the pasta and cook according to package instructions until just before al dente. Reserve ¼ cup of the pasta water and drain, then return the pasta to the pot off the heat.

2. Heat the avocado oil in a medium pot over medium-high heat. When it shimmers, add the ground beef and cook, breaking up the beef with a wooden spoon, 3 to 5 minutes, until somewhat browned. Reduce the heat to medium and stir in the carrots, celery, onions, and salt. Cook until the onions are translucent, about 10 minutes. Add the tomato paste and cook for 2 minutes, until slightly darker in color, then add the crushed tomatoes, nutmeg, coconut milk, red wine, and garlic. Reduce the heat to low and gently simmer for 10 minutes, until the sauce thickens.

3. Add the pasta to the simmering Bolognese sauce, and stir in the reserved pasta cooking water. Cook for 1 to 2 minutes, or until al dente. Divide between 2 bowls and serve immediately.

Indian-Spiced Root Vegetable Gratin with Crunchy Cashew Topping

Serves 2

FOR THE GRATIN

1 pound mixed root vegetables (beets, sweet potatoes, parsnips)

1 teaspoon fine-grain sea salt

2 tablespoons ghee or coconut oil, plus more for greasing the pan

1 small yellow onion, finely chopped

1 teaspoon ground ginger

1 teaspoon garam masala

½ teaspoon ground turmeric

1 teaspoon curry powder

3 garlic cloves, minced

1 cup canned full-fat coconut milk

1 teaspoon fresh lemon juice

2 tablespoons rice flour

1 cup fresh spinach, roughly chopped

Chopped fresh cilantro, to garnish (optional)

FOR THE TOPPING

¼ cup raw cashews

¼ cup unsweetened coconut flakes

¼ teaspoon fine-grain sea salt

2 garlic cloves

¼ teaspoon ground turmeric

¼ teaspoon ground ginger

1 teaspoon ghee or coconut oil

While I love the creamy texture and crispy top of classic potato gratin, I've always found the flavor a bit uninspiring. I decided to use coconut milk as a way to make a creamy filling without dairy, and, in doing so, found myself inspired to go for an Indian vibe in the rest of the dish, too. The garam masala, curry, and turmeric have tons of anti-inflammatory benefits and an unbeatable savory-sweet flavor. You can use whatever root vegetables you like, but combining beets, sweet potatoes, and parsnips gives a gorgeous, sunset-like color effect. The crunchy cashew-coconut topping that replaces cheese on top is so good you'll want to eat it plain (which I definitely encourage—it makes a delicious savory granola). A loaf pan makes this the perfect two-person gratin, but this is a great recipe to double or even triple. If you're making this with a partner, have one of you chop the vegetables and make the topping, while the other cooks the filling.

1. Preheat the oven to 350°F. Grease a 9 × 5-inch loaf pan.

2. Make the gratin: Peel the vegetables. Using a mandoline or a very sharp knife, thinly slice the vegetables into ⅛-inch-thick slices. In a large bowl, toss the sliced vegetables with ½ teaspoon of salt.

3. In a small pot, melt the ghee over medium heat. Add the onions and cook, stirring occasionally, until softened, about 5 minutes. Add the ginger, garam masala, turmeric, curry powder, garlic, and remaining ½ teaspoon of salt, and cook until fragrant, 1 to 2 minutes. Add the coconut milk and lemon juice and bring just to a boil, then reduce the heat to a simmer. Whisk in the rice flour, about ½ tablespoon at a time. Continue whisking until the mixture has thickened, about 1 minute. Taste and add more salt as needed, then remove the pot from the heat.

4. Meanwhile, **make the topping:** Pulse the cashews, coconut flakes, salt, garlic, turmeric, ginger, and ghee in a food processor a few times, until crumbly. (If you don't have a food processor, finely chop the garlic, then place everything in a zip-top bag and beat the crap out of it with a rolling pin.)

5. Assemble the gratin: Spoon enough sauce to cover the bottom of the prepared pan, about ¼ cup. Add a layer of root vegetables and a sprinkle of spinach, then add more sauce, more root vegetables, and more spinach—repeat until all the ingredients are used up and you have 8 to 10 layers. Sprinkle the topping on top.

6. Cover the pan loosely with foil and bake until the vegetables are fork-tender, 1¼ to 1½ hours. Remove the pan from the oven and take off the foil. Increase the temperature to 400°F, then bake the gratin for another 5 to 10 minutes, until the top is golden brown (watch it closely!). Let it cool for a few minutes, then slice into squares before dividing between 2 plates and topping with cilantro, if desired.

Zucchini Latkes with Apple-Rosemary Compote

Serves 2

FOR THE COMPOTE

2 Fuji, Gala, Granny Smith, or Honeycrisp apples, cored and chopped into 1-inch cubes

¼ teaspoon fine-grain sea salt

3 sprigs fresh rosemary

1 teaspoon fresh lemon juice

FOR THE LATKES

1 pound zucchini

1 medium yellow onion

1½ teaspoons fine-grain sea salt

2 large eggs, beaten

2 teaspoons arrowroot powder

¼ cup rice flour

Avocado oil or ghee, for frying

Freshly ground black pepper

I've always wanted to try zucchini latkes for a more nutrient-packed version of the classic potato version enjoyed at Hanukkah, but without the starch of the potatoes, the crispy exterior is difficult to achieve. Here I draw out as much moisture as possible from the watery zucchinis, then add arrowroot, an anti-inflammatory, gut-soothing, tuber-derived powder, to up the proportion of starch. The result? A latke that beats the ones from my favorite Jewish delis (shhh, don't tell them!). The sweet, woody, apple-rosemary compote adds extra phytochemicals and a sophisticated, addictive flavor. I prefer to leave the skins on the apples in my compote, as they add additional nutrients, and a rustic texture (plus, red apples make for a pink finished product!), but feel free to remove them if you prefer something smoother. If you're cooking this with a partner, one of you can handle the latkes while the other makes the compote.

1. **Make the compote:** Combine the apples, salt, and ¼ cup of water in a small pot over medium heat, then tuck the rosemary into the apples, making sure it's completely covered. Bring to a simmer, then reduce the heat to low. Cover and cook for 20 to 25 minutes, until the apples have reduced and become mushy. Remove the rosemary sprigs and discard (it's okay if a few leaves stay behind). Mash the apples with a spoon so they're saucy, but still textured. If the sauce is too liquidy, let it cook uncovered until it reaches your desired consistency, then stir in the lemon juice and set aside.

2. While the compote is simmering, **make the latkes:** Grate the zucchini and onion using a food processor fitted with the shredding disk or the large holes on a box grater. Transfer to a large bowl and toss with 1 teaspoon of salt. Let sit for 10 minutes to draw out water, then transfer the mixture to a thin, clean kitchen towel or a nut milk bag

and, over the sink, wring out as much liquid as possible. Return the zucchini and onion to the bowl, then mix in the eggs, the remaining ½ teaspoon of salt, the arrowroot powder, and the rice flour.

3. In a large skillet, heat enough oil to cover the bottom of the pan over medium heat until a bit of batter dropped in the oil sizzles. Drop the batter into the oil by the tablespoonful, pressing lightly to flatten the latkes. Fry the latkes for 2 to 3 minutes on each side, until golden brown. Top with compote and freshly ground pepper and serve.

Zack's Chicken Potpie

Serves 2

FOR THE CRUST

⅓ cup almond flour

⅓ cup coconut flour

¼ teaspoon freshly ground
black pepper

¼ teaspoon baking soda

4 tablespoons (½ stick) unsalted butter
from grass-fed cows or coconut oil,
frozen (see sidebar page 50)

3 tablespoons ice water

FOR THE FILLING

1 boneless, skinless chicken thigh,
cut into ½-inch cubes (about ⅔ cup)

1 tablespoon almond flour

½ teaspoon paprika

2 teaspoons fresh thyme leaves

¼ teaspoon fine-grain sea salt

¼ teaspoon freshly ground black pepper

3 tablespoons avocado or olive oil

1 medium onion, chopped

1 medium leek, white and light green
parts only, thinly sliced

1 medium carrot, finely chopped

¾ cup chopped shiitake mushrooms

½ cup frozen peas

1 cup chicken stock

1 tablespoon apple cider vinegar

¼ cup chopped fresh flat-leaf parsley

1 medium egg, beaten

Just as Picasso had a blue period, Zack had a pie period. He grew obsessed with piecrusts, and our weekends became filled with pastries and tarts (I wasn't complaining). His version of a chicken potpie was my absolute favorite. Instead of containing a wan, creamy filling, his is broth-based, with brighter, bolder flavors and just the right amount of vegetables. While his original had a spelt crust, we worked together to create the almond- and coconut-flour version here, and it's as amazing as you'd expect from anyone who had a pie period. If you're baking this with a partner, one of you can put together the crust while the other makes the filling.

1. **Make the crust:** Combine the almond flour, coconut flour, black pepper, and baking soda in a large bowl. Using a box grater, grate the butter into the flour. Using a pastry cutter (or 2 butter knives), chop the butter into the flour until the mixture resembles a coarse meal. Add the ice water, 1 tablespoon at a time, mixing with your hands as you go until the dough just holds together. Separate the dough into 2 pieces and shape into balls. Wrap each ball in plastic wrap and place in the fridge for at least 10 minutes and up to 24 hours.

2. **Make the filling:** Place the chicken, almond flour, paprika, thyme, salt, and pepper in a large zip-top bag, and shake well to coat. Heat 2 tablespoons of oil in a large, heavy-bottomed pot over medium heat. When it shimmers, add the onions and leeks, and sauté until translucent, 3 to 5 minutes. Add the carrots, mushrooms, and frozen peas and cook for 3 to 4 more minutes, until the mushrooms have lost a bit of moisture and begun to lightly brown. Add another tablespoon of oil and the chicken. Cook, stirring constantly, until the chicken is brown, scraping up the browned bits from the bottom,

(recipe continues)

7 to 10 minutes. Add the stock and apple cider vinegar. Bring to a boil, then reduce the heat to medium-low. Simmer until the liquid thickens, about 10 minutes. Add the parsley. Remove the pot from the heat and ladle the filling into two 6-ounce glass or ceramic ramekins.

3. Preheat the oven to 400°F.

4. Remove the dough balls from the fridge and place 1 of them between 2 pieces of wax or parchment paper. Using the heels of your hands or a rolling pin, gently press out into a circle a little larger than the ramekins. Repeat with the second ball.

5. Remove the top pieces of paper and carefully flip 1 dough round onto the top of each ramekin. Brush the beaten egg on top of the crusts. Bake for 15 minutes, until the crusts are golden brown. Let cool for 10 minutes before serving.

Cardamom Apple Turkey Meatballs with Mashed Parsnip "Potatoes" & Cranberry Gravy

Serves 2

FOR THE MEATBALLS

½ pound ground turkey
(85–94 percent lean)

½ cup grated apple (from 1 small apple)

1 medium egg

¼ cup almond flour

¾ teaspoon ground cumin

¾ teaspoon ground cardamom

½ teaspoon ground cinnamon

2 teaspoons finely chopped
fresh sage leaves

½ teaspoon fine-grain sea salt

Generous pinch of freshly ground
black pepper

1 tablespoon avocado oil

FOR THE CRANBERRY SAUCE

2 cups fresh or frozen cranberries

Grated zest and juice of 1 orange

½ teaspoon ground cinnamon

¼ teaspoon fine-grain sea salt

1 star anise (optional)

3 tablespoons coconut sugar

This dish combines the best of one of the least healthy, but very much together, American holidays—Thanksgiving—with a subtly Scandinavian flavor profile that elevates the entire dish and adds a drool-worthy, sweetly savory note. The phytonutrient-rich apples and spices make for the moistest, most flavorful meatball you've ever had, and the parsnips have an almost spiced cinnamon or nutmeg flavor that brings out the cardamom in the meatballs. I prefer my cranberry sauce fairly tart, but feel free to add more sugar if you'd like—we're using low-glycemic, high-mineral coconut sugar here, so your body won't hate you. If you're making this with a partner, one of you can tackle the meatballs, while the other cooks the cranberry sauce and parsnips.

1. **Make the meatballs:** Preheat the oven to 375°F. Line a rimmed baking sheet with parchment paper.

2. In a large bowl, combine the turkey, apple, egg, almond flour, cumin, cardamom, cinnamon, sage, salt, pepper, and avocado oil. Using 2 spoons or your hands, mix until well combined. Roll into 1½-inch balls, using your hands, and arrange the meatballs on the prepared baking sheet. Bake for 20 to 25 minutes, until the bottoms are brown and the insides are no longer pink.

3. Meanwhile, **make the cranberry sauce:** In a medium saucepan, bring the cranberries, orange zest and juice, cinnamon, salt, star anise (if using), and coconut sugar to a boil over medium heat. Reduce the heat to low and simmer, covered, for 10 to 15 minutes, or until most

(recipe continues)

FOR THE MASHED PARSNIPS

1 pound parsnips, diced

6 garlic cloves

Fine-grain sea salt

2 tablespoons olive oil

½ cup unsweetened cashew, hemp, or almond milk

¼ teaspoon freshly ground pepper

¼ cup roughly chopped chives, plus more to garnish

cranberries have popped. Remove the pan from the heat and discard the star anise. Let the sauce cool slightly, then transfer to a food processor or blender, and process until combined, but not completely smooth. (You could also use an immersion blender to do this right in the pan.)

4. Make the mashed parsnips: Place the parsnips and garlic in a large pot and cover with cold water. Add a small palmful of salt and bring to a boil over high heat. Cover, reduce the heat to medium, and simmer until the parsnips are fork-tender, about 8 minutes. Drain the parsnips and garlic (but do not rinse). Transfer to a food processor or blender (for a creamier texture) or a large bowl (for a more rustic finish). Pulse or mash the parsnips and garlic, then pulse or mash in the olive oil, milk, pepper, and chives. Taste and add more salt and pepper as needed.

5. To serve: Divide the mashed parsnips between 2 plates. Top with the meatballs, a generous amount of cranberry sauce, and some chives and freshly ground pepper. Serve immediately.

Fully Loaded Baked Potato-less Soup

Serves 2

FOR THE SOUP

3 cups (¾-inch pieces) scrubbed sunchokes, eyes removed

3 tablespoons avocado oil, ghee, or olive oil

½ teaspoon fine-grain sea salt

1 large yellow onion, sliced very thinly

2½ cups vegetable broth

¼ cup hulled hemp seeds

FOR THE TOPPINGS (OPTIONAL)

Fresh chives, chopped

Cooked pastured bacon, roughly chopped

Coconut bacon (recipe follows), broken into bits

Grated raw, grass-fed cheddar cheese

A few heaping spoonfuls nutritional yeast

There was a baked potato bar at my childhood mall that was my favorite after-school hangout. This recipe hits all the same satisfying notes as the ones of my youth, sans the massive stomachache. If you're not familiar with sunchokes (also called Jerusalem artichokes), the knobby roots are one of the most potent prebiotics around. This means they feed the good bacteria in your stomach—critical for good gut health. This soup is great on its own (it gets its creamy, buttery quality from the protein-rich hemp seeds), but it really takes on its fully loaded baked potato quality when heaped with toppings. Because being Healthier Together doesn't always mean being the same, I've provided options, so go with your (now well-fed) gut—although if you haven't tried coconut bacon, I highly recommend it. If you're making this with a partner, one of you can prepare the toppings while the other readies the soup.

1. Preheat the oven to 375°F.

2. Toss the sunchokes with 2 tablespoons of oil and ¼ teaspoon of salt on a parchment paper–lined baking sheet until well coated. Arrange in a single layer so the chokes are not touching each other. Bake, tossing occasionally, until fork-tender, 35 to 45 minutes.

3. Meanwhile, heat the remaining 1 tablespoon of oil in a heavy-bottomed medium pot over medium heat. When it shimmers, add the onions and the remaining ¼ teaspoon of salt. Cook, stirring occasionally, until the edges just begin to brown, about 10 minutes, then reduce the heat to low and continue to caramelize the onions, stirring occasionally, for 20 to 30 minutes, or until the sunchokes are finished roasting. Add the sunchokes and vegetable broth to the pot, increase the heat to high, and bring to a boil. Reduce the heat to low and simmer until the sunchokes fall apart when pierced with a fork, about 5 minutes.

4. Transfer half the sunchokes to a medium bowl, using a slotted spoon. Transfer the remaining sunchokes and liquid to a blender (you could also use an immersion blender to do this right in the pot; just remove half the mixture first). Add the hemp seeds and blend until very smooth. Add the reserved sunchokes and pulse until they are incorporated, with some texture remaining. Top as desired and enjoy.

Coconut Bacon

Makes about 1 cup

1 cup unsweetened coconut flakes

2 teaspoons avocado oil

1¼ teaspoons smoked paprika

2 teaspoons maple syrup

½ teaspoon liquid smoke (optional)

1 tablespoon tamari or soy sauce

¼ teaspoon fine-grain sea salt

¼ teaspoon freshly ground black pepper

Preheat the oven to 325°F.

On a parchment paper–lined baking sheet, toss together the coconut flakes, avocado oil, smoked paprika, maple syrup, liquid smoke, tamari, salt, and pepper until the coconut is well coated. Arrange in a single layer and bake for 10 minutes, tossing halfway through, until golden brown.

Remove from the oven and let cool completely (it will continue to crisp up as it cools). Store at room temperature in an airtight container for up to a week.

Slow-Cooker Short Rib Chocolate Chili with Jalapeño Cornbread Polenta

Serves 2

FOR THE CHILI

1 pound bone-in beef short ribs

Fine-grain sea salt

2 tablespoons avocado oil, ghee, or olive oil

2 medium carrots, diced

1 medium yellow onion, diced

2 celery stalks, diced

3 tablespoons tomato paste

1 tablespoon chili powder

1 teaspoon ground cumin

1 teaspoon dried oregano

1 teaspoon ground cinnamon

1 cup vegetable broth

3 garlic cloves, minced

1 (14.5-ounce) can stewed tomatoes

2 tablespoons raw cacao powder

1 small sweet potato, chopped into ½-inch cubes

2 cups chopped curly kale, stems removed

1 (15-ounce) can black beans, drained and rinsed

Juice of ½ lime

Cornbread Polenta (recipe follows)

2 green onions, white and light green parts only, thinly sliced

Is there anything better than coming home on a freezing-cold day and knowing you have hot chili waiting for you? This recipe uses short ribs almost as a topping, to add flavor and texture to the heaps of sweet potato and kale (although you can easily make this recipe vegan by omitting the short ribs and adding another two cups of beans). As a lover of all carbs, it's no surprise that my favorite part of this dish is the corn- and jalapeño-studded, pan-fried polenta (I'm drooling already), which mimics cornbread in texture and flavor, but has no flour or sugar. It's honestly better than traditional cornbread, especially when topped with the umami-rich, tomatoey, just chocolatey enough chili. If you're making this with a partner, one person can finish up the chili while the other makes the cornbread polenta.

1. Make the chili: Sprinkle the short ribs with a generous amount of salt. Heat a heavy-bottomed medium skillet over medium-high heat until very hot, about 2 minutes. Add 1 tablespoon of oil. Add the short ribs and sear for 1 to 2 minutes per side, until lightly brown and crusted.

2. Transfer the ribs to a slow cooker. Carefully wipe out the pan (it will be hot!) and return it to medium heat. Add the remaining 1 tablespoon of oil to the skillet. When the oil shimmers, add the carrots, onions, celery, and 1 teaspoon of salt. Cook for 2 to 3 minutes, stirring occasionally, until the onions are lightly brown, then add the tomato paste, chili powder, cumin, oregano, and cinnamon. Cook for 1 to 2 minutes, until the spices are

(recipe continues)

fragrant, then transfer to the slow cooker, along with the vegetable broth, garlic, and stewed tomatoes. Cook on low for 7 to 8 hours (or on high for 4 hours, if you're in a hurry).

3. Remove the short ribs from the slow cooker. Pull the meat off the bones and shred with a fork. Return the meat to the slow cooker and add the cacao, sweet potatoes, kale, and black beans. Cook on low for an additional 20 to 30 minutes, or until the sweet potatoes are fork-tender. Turn off the heat and squeeze in the lime juice. Taste and add more salt as needed.

4. Serve the chili over the cornbread polenta, topped with the green onions.

Cornbread Polenta

Makes 6 pieces

2 to 3 tablespoons avocado oil, ghee or olive oil

¾ cup fresh or frozen corn, thawed

1 jalapeño, seeded and minced

½ teaspoon fine-grain sea salt

2 garlic cloves, minced

2 cups vegetable broth

½ cup coarsely ground cornmeal or polenta

Heat 2 tablespoons of oil in a medium, heavy-bottomed pot over medium-high heat. Add the corn, jalapeño, and salt, and cook, stirring occasionally, until the corn is lightly browned, 3 to 5 minutes for fresh corn, 5 to 7 minutes for frozen. Add the garlic and vegetable broth and bring to a boil. Slowly add the cornmeal, whisking vigorously and continuously to keep clumps from forming.

Reduce the heat to low and cover. Cook for 15 to 20 minutes, stirring occasionally to prevent lumps. When the mixture is creamy, remove the pot from the heat and stir in additional salt to taste.

Serve as is, under the chili or, for more authentic cornbread vibes, press into a loaf pan until about 1 inch thick. Let cool completely in the fridge and cut into 2-inch squares. Heat the remaining 1 tablespoon of oil in a large skillet over medium heat until it shimmers, then fry each piece for 2 to 3 minutes per side, until golden brown.

Cheese Your Own Adventure

Just because you're doing this Healthier Together thing doesn't mean you have to (or should!) agree on everything. The best way to stick to a healthier lifestyle is to allow room for flexibility, which brings us to this cheese-venture. You'll start off by making a simple "cheese" sauce, which contains no actual cheese (plot twist!), but plenty of vitamin A, fiber, B vitamins, and protein . . . basically, unlike the gooey Velveeta stuff this sauce so closely resembles in taste and texture, it's incredibly nourishing and healthful. Based on what you're each craving, use it to top, drizzle, smother, and toss with any of the other meal components on the next page.

World's Best Cheese Sauce

Serves 2

1 cup diced carrots (from 2 small carrots)

2 cups peeled, diced russet potatoes (from 1 large potato)

¼ teaspoon fine-grain sea salt, plus more for the water

¾ teaspoon tamari or soy sauce

1 teaspoon onion powder

½ teaspoon garlic powder

½ teaspoon smoked paprika

3 tablespoons nutritional yeast

3 tablespoons unsweetened almond, hemp, or cashew milk

½ teaspoon fresh thyme leaves, chopped

1. In a medium pot, cover the carrots and potatoes with cold water by 1 inch. Add a small palmful of salt and bring to a boil over high heat. Boil until fork-tender, 15 to 20 minutes. Reserve ¼ cup of the cooking liquid, then drain the vegetables (but do not rinse) and let them cool slightly.

2. Transfer the vegetables to a blender or food processor and add the tamari, onion powder, garlic powder, smoked paprika, salt, nutritional yeast, milk, and half the thyme leaves. Blend or process on high for at least 1 minute, scraping down the sides as necessary. If you're having trouble getting things moving, add the reserved cooking water 1 tablespoon at a time. Be sure to blend for the full minute, even if the mixture seems smooth already, so that the starches release from the potatoes to achieve the correct texture. Pulse in the remaining thyme leaves until evenly distributed, but little green flecks remain.

NOTE: The following variations serve 1 (not 2), so you can cheese your own adventure. If you and your partner want the same dish, double the recipe!

(recipe continues)

You're in the mood for something super-filling, but that won't leave you feeling *so* full that you feel sick.

You're feeling pretty healthy tonight. I mean, not that healthy (you're making cheese sauce, after all), but you're ready for some cruciferous action in your life.

Loaded Baked Potato

Scrub and pat dry 1 medium potato or 1 sweet potato (I like white russet potatoes, which, despite their bad rap, are a great source of fiber and potassium, but you do you). Pierce the skin with a fork a few times, then bake at 400°F for 40 to 60 minutes, or until fork-tender. Meanwhile, chop up a green onion (white and light green parts only) and fry a piece of pastured bacon (if desired)—I prefer cooking it over super-low heat in a pan for maximum crispiness (you can also prep some Coconut Bacon, page 67). Chop the bacon, then cut the potato in half. Top your tater with half the cheese sauce, a sprinkle of green onion, bacon, and a generous amount of salt and pepper.

Roasted Broccoli
with Cheese Sauce, Chipotle and Toasted Pepitas

Chop a small bunch of broccoli into florets. Drizzle with high-heat oil and a generous sprinkle of fine-grain sea salt, and roast on a baking sheet at 400°F until the edges just begin to turn brown and crispy, about 15 minutes. Meanwhile, toast up a handful of pepitas in a small pan over low heat until golden brown, about 5 minutes. To serve, drizzle the broccoli with cheese sauce, shake on some chipotle powder, and sprinkle with toasted pepitas. Add some black pepper to taste and dig in.

You want something
a little zesty, a little
creamy, a little spicy.

You want hearty comfort
food that'll take you straight
back to childhood.

Better-Than-Bar-Food Nachos

Drain and rinse 1 (15-ounce) can of black beans, then warm them up in a small pot over low heat, stirring constantly, about 4 minutes. Chop a green onion (white and light green parts only) and a handful of cilantro, and open a jar of salsa. Quarter a lime. Spread some tortilla chips in a single layer on a plate, then liberally drizzle them with half the cheese sauce before loading on your toppings. Finish with some sea salt and pepper to taste.

Mac 'n' Cheese

Boil a medium pot of water with a small palmful of fine-grain sea salt. Cook 1 serving of your favorite pasta until al dente. Drain. Toss the pasta with half the cheese sauce until well coated, then sprinkle with a bit of black pepper, paprika, and chopped fresh thyme (if you're feeling fancy).

Better Than Takeout

As a New Yorker, I have many friends who eat takeout almost every night, and one who even, when having a dinner party, emails a restaurant menu for everyone to choose from beforehand. You don't need me to remind you, but takeout meals often contain some of the most unhealthy ingredients around—chefs boost flavor through copious amounts of sugar and inflammatory vegetable oils, and often these meals don't even taste that good. The recipes in this section mimic the vibes of takeout staples but they are way better—both for your body and for your taste buds. Try whipping one up with your partner on nights you're thinking about ordering in, and you'll never go back.

Zucchini Noodle Pad See Ew

Serves 2

FOR THE STEAK

5 ounces flank steak from grass-fed cattle, cut into ⅛-inch-thick, bite-size slices

½ teaspoon fine-grain sea salt

½ teaspoon tamari or soy sauce

1 teaspoon avocado oil

1 teaspoon coconut sugar

FOR THE STIR-FRY

2 medium zucchini

½ teaspoon fine-grain sea salt

⅓ cup raw cashews, roughly chopped

1 tablespoon plus 2 teaspoons avocado oil

1 tablespoon peeled, minced ginger

3 garlic cloves, minced

1 small bunch bok choy (½ to ¾ pound), chopped (leaves and stems separated)

2 tablespoons tamari or soy sauce

2 teaspoons rice vinegar

1 large egg, beaten

Sriracha, to serve (optional)

Pad see ew is my favorite Thai food takeout order—for me, it's all about those tangles of wide, flat noodles. I was working on an article about making vegetable noodles without a spiralizer when it hit me: the noodles you could create with a vegetable peeler were literally the same width as those in my beloved pad see ew. The zucchini noodles are tossed with a gingery, garlicky brown sauce (ahh, the delicious brown sauces of Thai takeout); you won't miss their carby counterparts. If you want a veg version of this, simply omit the beef—it's plenty filling with just the eggs and the cashews. If you're cooking it with a partner, one of you can marinate the steak and handle the zucchini noodles while the other works on the stir-fry itself.

1. **Marinate the steak:** Combine the steak, salt, tamari, avocado oil, and coconut sugar in a large zip-top plastic bag. Shake to coat and marinate at room temperature for at least 20 minutes or in the refrigerator for up to 24 hours.

2. **Make the zucchini noodles:** Use a vegetable peeler to slice the zucchini into long, thin ribbons—I like to cut a small piece, lengthwise, off the bottom of the zucchini so it rests it flat on the cutting board, then hold it long-side down and drag the peeler toward me. Place the zucchini noodles in a strainer set over a bowl or in the sink and sprinkle with salt, tossing to coat. Let drain for at least 10 minutes or up to 30. Pat the noodles dry with a clean kitchen towel.

3. Heat a dry wok or large skillet over medium heat. Place the cashews in the dry skillet and toast, stirring frequently, until the smallest pieces have turned golden brown, about 3 minutes. Remove the cashews from the pan.

(recipe continues)

4. Return the pan to medium-high heat and add
1 tablespoon of oil. When it shimmers, add the ginger,
garlic, bok choy stems, tamari, and 2 tablespoons of water,
and cook, stirring frequently, for about 4 minutes, until the
bok choy is crisp-tender. Add the bok choy leaves and rice
vinegar and cook until the leaves wilt, 1 to 2 minutes. Push
everything to one side of the pan and add the egg to the
other; cook until almost set, then toss with the vegetables
to combine. Transfer to a medium bowl.

5. Wipe out the pan, return it to medium-high heat, and
add the remaining 2 teaspoons of oil. When it shimmers,
add the beef, allowing the excess marinade to drip off it as
you pull it out. Cook, stirring frequently, until seared on
the outside and not quite cooked through, about 4 minutes.
Add the zucchini noodles to the pan and toss to coat with
the oil in the pan (I like to use 2 wooden spoons to do this).
Spread the noodles out in the pan and let them cook for
a minute or two, until they just begin to brown. Turn the
heat off. Add the bok choy and egg mixture back to the pan
and use your spoons to toss until the noodles are coated
and all the ingredients are well distributed.

6. Divide the pad see ew between 2 plates and top with the
toasted cashews and sriracha, if desired, to serve.

Chicken & Butternut Squash Tikka Masala with Super-Fresh Mint Cilantro Chutney

Serves 2

FOR THE CHUTNEY

1-Inch piece of ginger, peeled and roughly chopped

½ jalapeño, seeded

3 garlic cloves

1½ cups loosely packed fresh cilantro leaves

1½ cups fresh mint leaves

Juice of 1 lemon

1 teaspoon honey

½ teaspoon fine-grain sea salt

TIP: To make this recipe vegan, omit the chicken and skip straight from cooking the butternut squash to adding the onions and ginger. When you add the coconut milk, add 1 (15-ounce) can of drained, rinsed chickpeas and proceed as directed.

My divorced parents, who agreed on little in life, both proclaimed a deep hatred of Indian food—it was "too heavy" and "smelled unfamiliar." Well, I won them *both* over with this revamped tikka masala, which bulks up the chicken with sweet butternut squash and subs coconut milk for gut-irritating heavy cream. The secret, though, is the chutney—herby and light and impossibly zesty, and it turns a traditionally rich dish into something cravably fresh. You'll want to spoon *a lot* of it on top; it's the magic that brings the dish to life. You can eat this on its own, or serve it on top of rice (I love using black forbidden rice for its beautiful color and slightly nutty flavor) or with a side of naan. If you're making this with a partner, one of you can handle the chutney while the other makes the tikka masala.

1. **Make the chutney:** In a food processor, blend together the ginger, jalapeño, garlic, cilantro, mint, lemon juice, honey, salt, and 1 tablespoon of water until smooth, with some texture remaining. Add more water, 1 tablespoon at a time, if needed to reach your desired consistency.

2. **Make the tikka masala:** Toss the chicken with 1 teaspoon of garam masala, ½ teaspoon of salt, and the pepper in a medium bowl. Set aside to marinate while you cook the butternut squash.

3. Heat 1 tablespoon oil in a large skillet over medium-high heat. When it shimmers, add the squash and ¼ teaspoon of salt, and toss until well coated. Spread the squash into an even layer and cook, without stirring, until golden

(recipe continues)

FOR THE TIKKA MASALA

½ pound boneless, skinless chicken breasts or thighs, cut into 1-inch cubes

3 teaspoons garam masala

1¼ teaspoons fine-grain sea salt

¼ teaspoon freshly ground black pepper

2 to 3 tablespoons high-heat oil

2 cups (¾-inch cubes) butternut squash (about ½ small butternut squash)

½ medium yellow onion, chopped

1-inch piece of ginger, peeled and minced

¼ cup tomato paste

1½ teaspoons ground turmeric

Generous pinch of cayenne pepper

1 (13.5-ounce) can full-fat coconut milk

2 garlic cloves, minced

1 cup frozen peas, thawed and drained

Naan or cooked rice, to serve (optional)

brown on the bottom, about 5 minutes. Reduce the heat to low and cover. Cook for 7 to 15 minutes more, until fork-tender but not falling apart (smaller pieces will cook faster). Transfer to a medium bowl.

4. Heat another 1 tablespoon of oil in the same skillet (no need to wipe it clean) over medium-high heat. Add the chicken and cook, stirring occasionally, until lightly browned and cooked through, about 5 minutes. Using a slotted spoon, transfer the chicken to the bowl with the butternut squash, leaving as much oil in the pan as possible.

5. Return the skillet to medium heat and add a bit more oil to the pan as needed to coat the bottom. Add the onions, ginger, and the remaining ½ teaspoon salt (if there are brown bits stuck to the pan from the chicken, add water 1 tablespoon at a time, scraping to deglaze). Cook, stirring occasionally, until the onions are soft and translucent, about 3 minutes, adding another tablespoon of water at a time if anything sticks. Add the tomato paste, turmeric, cayenne, and remaining 2 teaspoons of garam masala and cook, stirring constantly, until the spices are fragrant, about 30 seconds. Add the coconut milk and garlic and keep stirring until the sauce comes to a simmer. Cook until it reduces by about a third, about 10 minutes. Return the chicken and butternut squash to the pan, add the peas, and cook until warmed through, about a minute more.

6. Remove the pan from the heat. Divide the tikki masala between 2 bowls, top with a generous portion of chutney, and serve with naan or rice, if desired.

Caramelized Onion, Beet & Beef Sliders

Serves 2

FOR THE SLIDERS

2 tablespoons avocado oil

1 medium yellow onion, roughly chopped

1 cup shredded raw beets
(from 1 medium peeled beet)

¼ teaspoon fine-grain sea salt

½ pound ground beef (preferably from grass-fed cattle)

1 medium egg

1 teaspoon tamari or soy sauce

6 slider buns or large romaine leaves

FOR THE TOPPINGS (OPTIONAL)

Grainy mustard

Sliced avocado

Sliced red onion

Pickles

Quick-Pickled Crudités (page 145)

TIP: Is grilling healthy? Unfortunately, not really. Those black marks on your food (which are why we're grilling in the first place) are physical signs of carcinogens. You can help protect your body from carcinogens by adding protective elements to your grilled food (like rosemary and garlic), but rather than stressing about it, I choose to grill very occasionally, and I make it worth it. On a perfect summer day, surrounded by friends, I'll toss something on the grill and enjoy it; otherwise, I'll pan-sear on the stove. What you do regularly matters far more than what you do occasionally.

I've had veggie burgers made with beets, which I find too earthy and structurally disastrous (they fall apart!), and I've had beef burgers that always leave me wanting more veggies. Here the two come together with guest star caramelized onion for a burger that's out-of-this-world delicious. There's a subtle sweetness (you don't even need ketchup!), and a delightful savory quality, amped up by the addition of tamari. While you can grill these, I prefer them pan-fried for health reasons (see Tip) and because it makes them easy enough for a weeknight dinner.

1. Heat 1 tablespoon of oil in a medium skillet over medium-high heat. When it shimmers, add the onions and cook, stirring occasionally, until they just begin to brown, 3 to 5 minutes. Reduce the heat to low and cook, stirring occasionally, for 15 minutes until the onions are evenly browned and softened. Add the beets and salt, and continue to cook on low for 15 minutes, until the beets are lightly browned. Let them cool slightly, then transfer them to a medium bowl. Add the beef, egg, and tamari, and mix until combined.

2. Using your hands, roll the mixture into 2-inch balls, flattening them slightly with your palm. Wipe out the skillet and return it to medium-low heat. Add the remaining tablespoon of oil to the skillet and when it shimmers, add the burgers, working in batches as needed. Cook for 3 to 4 minutes per side, until browned (it'll still look a bit pink because of the beet, but that's okay).

3. Serve on buns or wrapped in romaine, with your desired toppings.

Mexican Street Corn & Quinoa Bowl

Serves 2

½ cup uncooked quinoa

1 cup vegetable broth

2 tablespoons plain hummus, at room temperature

1 teaspoon chili powder, plus more for garnish

1 garlic clove, minced

4 tablespoons ghee, melted

½ teaspoon fine-grain sea salt

2 tablespoons nutritional yeast

½ medium yellow onion, diced

2 ears of corn, kernels sliced from the cobs, or 1½ cups frozen corn, thawed

Grated zest and juice of 1 lime

½ cup fresh cilantro, roughly chopped, to garnish

1 green onion, white and light green parts only, roughly chopped

There's little better than proper Mexican street corn: the sweet crunch of the corn, creamy mayo, piquant garlic, and zesty lime all come together for a single, heavenly bite. How do you make that healthy? The genius of this recipe is in the hummus-based sauce, which is as creamy as mayo (and far more flavorful), but helps add protein that, along with the quinoa, turns this dish into a complete meal. This is one of Zack and my go-to weeknight dinners when we're feeling a bit uninspired by typical fare: it's unique enough to be interesting, hearty enough to be satisfying, and quick enough to be unintimidating and wholly doable, even on the busiest of days. If you're making this with a partner, have one of you cook the quinoa and prep the hummus sauce, while the other handles the corn-and-onion mixture.

1. Rinse the quinoa well. Combine the quinoa and vegetable broth in a small pot. Bring to a boil over medium-high heat, then cover and reduce the heat to low. Simmer for 15 minutes, or until all the liquid is absorbed. Remove the pot from the heat, uncover, and fluff the quinoa with a fork.

2. Meanwhile, in a small bowl, whisk together the hummus, chili powder, garlic, 2 tablespoons of ghee, ¼ teaspoon of salt, and nutritional yeast until smooth and creamy.

3. Heat the remaining 2 tablespoons of ghee in a large skillet over medium heat. Add the onions and corn and cook, stirring occasionally, until both are golden brown, 7 to 10 minutes. Remove the pan from the heat, and transfer to a medium bowl. Add the quinoa, lime juice and zest, and the remaining ¼ teaspoon of salt, and toss to combine well.

4. Divide the mixture evenly between 2 bowls, then top with the hummus mixture. Garnish with cilantro, green onion, and a sprinkle of chili powder.

Caribbean Crusted Fish & Plantain Chips with Avocado Tartar Sauce

Serves 2

FOR THE TARTAR SAUCE

2 garlic cloves

1 small jalapeño, seeded

1 medium ripe avocado, peeled and pitted

¼ cup nondairy yogurt or yogurt from milk from grass-fed cows

½ teaspoon fine-grain sea salt

2 tablespoons pickle juice

¼ cup dill, cilantro, flat-leaf parsley, or other fresh green herbs

¼ cup diced pickles (preferably fermented, from the refrigerated section of the store)

FOR THE FISH

2 medium plantains, cut into batons 2 to 3 inches long, ½ inch thick

2 tablespoons melted coconut oil

1 tablespoon plus 1 teaspoon sweet paprika

½ cup coconut flour

¼ cup raw hemp hearts

1 teaspoon dried thyme

½ teaspoon ground ginger

½ teaspoon garlic powder

½ teaspoon onion powder

For my British friends, fish and chips is a pub staple, but, of course, when I made it myself, I had to give it a little twist. Enter plantain chips—chips, of course, meaning fries. If plantains aren't in your cooking repertoire yet, get ready. These starchy cousins of banana are usually cooked before being eaten and are a great source of vitamin B_6 and magnesium. When you turn them into fries, you want them to have just the right crunch, so look for medium-ripe plantains—not green, but not yet completely black. Dip them in avocado tartar sauce (full of healthy fat and probiotics) and you have a nutrient-rich, healthy side. I like to bake the fish, but you can also fry it in a little bit of coconut oil for a more traditional experience. If you're making this with a partner, one of you can make the tartar sauce and plantains while the other preps the fish.

1. Preheat the oven to 350°F. Line 2 baking sheets with parchment paper.

2. Make the avocado tartar sauce: In a food processor or blender, pulse together the garlic and jalapeño until a chunky paste forms. Add the avocado, yogurt, salt, pickle juice, and herbs. Pulse until smooth. Pour the sauce into a small bowl and stir in the diced pickles. Cover with a piece of plastic wrap pressed directly onto the surface of the sauce (to prevent browning) and refrigerate until ready to use.

3. Make the fish: In a large bowl, toss the plantains with the coconut oil and 1 tablespoon of sweet paprika. Arrange on one of the prepared baking sheets so the plantains are not touching. Bake for 25 to 30 minutes, turning once or twice, until fork-tender and golden brown. Remove from the oven and let them cool a bit.

½ teaspoon ground allspice

¼ teaspoon ground white pepper

2 teaspoons coconut sugar

1 teaspoon fine-grain sea salt

¼ teaspoon cayenne pepper (optional)

1 medium egg, beaten

½ pound white fish, such as cod, tilapia, or catfish (see "What's the Deal with Buying Fish?" on page 183), cut into 1½-inch pieces

Lime wedges, to garnish

4. Meanwhile, combine the coconut flour, hemp hearts, remaining 1 teaspoon of paprika, thyme, ginger, garlic powder, onion powder, allspice, white pepper, coconut sugar, salt, and cayenne (if using) in a wide, shallow bowl, and stir with a fork until well blended. In a separate wide bowl or plate, whisk together the egg and 1 tablespoon of water.

5. Dip each piece of fish into the egg, allowing the excess to drip off, then into the flour mixture, turning to coat and pressing the flour into the fish to make sure it's completely covered. Place the breaded fish on the other prepared baking sheet. Bake for 20 to 25 minutes, flipping gently once, until the fish flakes easily with a fork.

6. Serve the fish and chips with the avocado tartar sauce alongside for dipping, garnished with lime wedges for squeezing.

Super-Quick Cast-Iron Pizza

Serves 2

Avocado oil, for greasing the pan

2 (10-inch) tortillas

4 tablespoons tomato sauce

Toppings of choice (cheese from the milk of grass-fed cows, thinly sliced vegetables, dried or fresh herbs)

Topping Options

CLASSIC NEW YORK
Mozzarella cheese from the milk of grass-fed cows + dried oregano + dried basil + garlic powder + salt

BETTER THAN MARGARITA
Chunks of mozzarella from the milk of grass-fed cows + fresh basil (add after cooking) + drizzle of hot honey (page 99, add after cooking)

BRUSSELS SPROUTS & BACON-ISH
Shredded Brussels sprouts pan-fried in avocado oil with a sprinkle of salt until just brown + cooked pasture-raised bacon or coconut bacon (page 67)

BBQ CHICKEN PARTY
Cheddar cheese from the milk of grass-fed cows + shredded pasture-raised rotisserie chicken tossed in BBQ sauce + thin-sliced red onions

THE SALAD PIZZA
Thinly sliced apple + toasted, chopped walnuts + fresh arugula (add after cooking) + a drizzle of olive oil (add after cooking) + a drizzle of balsamic vinegar (add after cooking)

This is more of a technique than a recipe (the flavor of the pizza itself is yours to customize, although the combos listed can get you started) but it's such a staple for Zack and me that I couldn't leave it out. Inspired by a J. Kenji López-Alt recipe, this combined stovetop and oven recipe results in a crisp-crust pizza that tastes exactly like Domino's thin crust, but is way healthier. You want to use high-quality tortillas (my favorites are the entire Siete grain-free range and the La Tortilla Factory gluten-free teff tortillas), and a pizza sauce that's organic and sugar-free. After that, the ball's in your court—add your favorite toppings and watch this very quickly replace your bad delivery habit.

1. Preheat oven to 425°F.

2. Drizzle a bit of avocado oil in a 10-inch cast-iron skillet and warm over medium-high heat, turning the pan to coat it evenly. When the oil shimmers, wipe out the excess oil and place one tortilla in the pan. Reduce heat to medium and let cook for one minute. Flip the tortilla and cook for an additional minute while you add 2 tablespoons of sauce, spreading it all the way to the tortilla's edge.

3. Remove the pan from the heat and add the toppings of your choice, reserving fresh herbs to finish. Transfer the pan to the oven and bake for 2 to 4 minutes, or until the edges of the tortilla are golden brown but not burned (if you're not using cheese, check on the early side). Transfer the pan back to the stove and cook for another 1 to 2 minutes over medium heat, until the bottom is browned, but not burned. Transfer the pizza to a plate and let it cool slightly. Top with fresh herbs, if using.

4. Repeat with second pizza and serve.

General Tso's Cauliflower

Serves 2

¾ cup rice flour

½ teaspoon garlic powder

¼ teaspoon ground ginger

Generous pinch fine-grain sea salt

1 medium head cauliflower,
cut into florets

1 tablespoon toasted sesame seed oil

1 tablespoon peeled, minced ginger

2 garlic cloves, minced

3 tablespoons tomato paste

¼ cup tamari or soy sauce

3 tablespoons rice vinegar

¼ cup vegetable broth

½ cup coconut sugar

1 green onion, white and light green
parts only, thinly sliced, to garnish

My friend Briana and I became addicted to General Tso's Cauliflower at a now-closed restaurant on New York City's Lower East Side, and one cold and boring winter's day, decided to try to re-create the recipe at home. After several hours, we emerged flour-covered but wholly satisfied with these crispy, sweet-and-sour bites. It's now one of my favorite ways to win over non-cauliflower lovers. You can double this recipe and serve it as an appetizer for a group, or keep it as is for an easy, healthy dinner (the lycopene-rich tomato paste, combined with the liver-detoxifying cauliflower, is exceptionally good for making skin glow). If you opt for the latter, I recommend serving the dish over rice, quinoa, or even cauliflower rice, if you're up for an all-caul dinner. If you're making this with a partner, have one of you prepare the cauliflower while the other whips up the sauce.

1. Preheat the oven to 425°F. Line a baking sheet (or 2, if you have them) with parchment paper.

2. In a large bowl, whisk together ½ cup of rice flour, ½ cup of water, the garlic powder, ground ginger, and salt. Dust the cauliflower with the remaining ¼ cup rice flour, then dredge the florets in the wet rice flour mixture until well coated, shaking off any excess. Arrange on the prepared baking sheet, spacing them apart. Bake for 25 to 40 minutes, flipping once halfway through, until golden brown all over (the smaller the florets, the faster they'll cook). Transfer to a large bowl. Keep the oven on and the lined baking sheet handy.

3. Heat the sesame oil in a small pot over medium heat. When it shimmers, add the ginger and garlic, and sauté, stirring constantly, until fragrant, 2 to 3 minutes. Add the tomato paste, tamari, rice vinegar, broth, and coconut sugar, whisking to combine. Bring to a boil, then reduce the heat to low and simmer, stirring occasionally, until reduced by about one-quarter, about 5 minutes.

4. Pour the sauce over the cauliflower and toss to coat well. Transfer the cauliflower back to the baking sheet and bake for an additional 10 to 15 minutes, or until the cauliflower is dark brown but not burned.

5. Serve topped with the green onions.

Falafel Flatbread

Serves 2

2 cups chickpea flour

1 teaspoon fine-grain sea salt

4 garlic cloves, minced

2 tablespoons finely chopped
fresh flat-leaf parsley

2 tablespoons finely chopped
fresh cilantro

1 teaspoon ground cumin

½ teaspoon ground coriander

¼ teaspoon chili powder

2 teaspoons fresh lemon juice

8 tablespoons avocado oil

TOPPINGS (OPTIONAL)

Red Pepper Muhammara
(recipe follows)

Yogurt

Toasted walnuts

Chopped fresh flat-leaf parsley

Tahini

Chopped cucumbers

Chopped tomatoes

Torn spinach

Chopped purple onion

Fresh lemon juice

Everyone loves falafel, but to truly make it taste good at home, you need to use dried chickpeas and soak them overnight—canned chickpeas don't produce the same results. I don't usually feel like going through that process (who has the patience?), but I realized that one of my favorite types of flatbread crusts, socca, is made with chickpea flour. Add the right seasoning and—boom!—instant falafel flavor. All the deliciousness, no soaking required. It pairs perfectly with a red pepper muhammara sauce, which is what your standard pizza sauce would taste like if it became heartier, more savory, and 80 times more complex and satisfying. Once you have the flatbread, you can individualize your pizza, Healthier Together–style, with custom topping blends. If you're cooking this with a partner, one of you can make the flatbreads while the other handles the muhammara.

1. In a large bowl, whisk together the chickpea flour, salt, garlic, parsley, cilantro, cumin, coriander, chili powder, lemon juice, 2 cups of water, and 6 tablespoons of avocado oil. Let the mixture soak for 30 to 60 minutes to hydrate the flour.

2. Preheat the broiler with the rack in the center position.

3. Place a 10-inch cast-iron skillet in the oven to heat up, about 5 minutes. Carefully remove the pan. Swirl in 1 tablespoon of avocado oil to coat the bottom, then pour in half the flatbread batter. Tilt the pan until the batter is evenly spread. Return the pan to the oven and broil for 3 to 5 minutes, until the edges are brown and toasty.

4. Remove the pan from the oven and gently slide the flatbread onto a plate. Repeat with the remaining batter.

5. Smear the flatbreads with muhammara and/or yogurt and top as desired.

(recipe continues)

Red Pepper Muhammara

Makes about 1½ cups

2 large red bell peppers, halved lengthwise and seeded

¾ cup raw walnuts

1½ teaspoons fresh lemon juice

2 tablespoons tomato paste

1 garlic clove

½ teaspoon ground cumin

½ teaspoon fine-grain sea salt

1 tablespoon pomegranate molasses

½ teaspoon Aleppo pepper flakes or red pepper flakes

¼ cup olive oil

Preheat the oven to 400°F.

Arrange the peppers on a parchment-lined baking sheet. Roast for 45 minutes to 1 hour, flipping once halfway through, until both sides are dark brown and spotted. You can also brown them over a gas stovetop using heat-proof tongs. Transfer to a large bowl and cover with plastic wrap. Let them steam for 10 to 15 minutes until the peppers are cool enough to handle, then use your fingers to gently remove their peels.

Meanwhile, spread out the walnuts on a parchment-lined baking sheet. Place in the oven with the peppers and toast for 2–3 minutes, or until golden brown (watch them closely!).

Transfer the peeled peppers and nuts to a food processor or blender. Add the lemon juice, tomato paste, garlic, cumin, salt, pomegranate molasses, pepper flakes, and olive oil, and process or blend into a smooth paste. Keep in the fridge in a tightly sealed container for up to 4 days.

Cornflake "Fried" Chicken with Hot Honey & Gut-Healing Sauerkraut Citrus Coleslaw

Serves 2

FOR THE CHICKEN

1 cup unsweetened almond milk

2 tablespoons apple cider vinegar

¾ teaspoon fine-grain sea salt

1 pound boneless, skinless chicken breasts, cut lengthwise into 4 strips

¾ cup cornflakes

¾ cup almond flour

¾ teaspoon paprika

¾ teaspoon freshly ground black pepper

Hot honey (store-bought or homemade, recipe follows)

FOR THE COLESLAW

1 cup raw, fermented sauerkraut (see Tip on page 99)

1 cup shredded carrot (from 1 large carrot)

½ jalapeño, seeded and minced

½ medium red onion, sliced

Grated zest and juice of 1 orange

2 tablespoons olive oil

¼ teaspoon fine-grain sea salt

2 teaspoons raw honey

When we got married on an organic farm in Sonoma, California, Zack and I knew we wanted to serve a cornucopia of fresh veggie-based dishes, with one meat option so no one would stage a riot. When we tasted the cornflake-crusted fried chicken with a hot honey drizzle, we were instantly smitten, and one of my fondest postwedding memories is eating the leftovers straight out of gallon-size zip-top bags in our hotel room. This version keeps all the deliciousness, but ups the health factor, with a nondairy buttermilk mixture that ensures the chicken stays incredibly moist, and an almond flour crust that bakes up crispy with no frying necessary. The coleslaw swaps traditional raw cabbage for sauerkraut, a potent gut healer that's filled with probiotics. With sweet and zesty orange and just a touch of jalapeño, it's the perfect refreshing side dish. If you're making this with a partner, have one of you prep the chicken while the other makes the coleslaw.

1. In a medium bowl, mix together the almond milk, apple cider vinegar, and ¼ teaspoon of sea salt. Add the chicken, ensuring it is submerged. Cover with plastic and chill in the fridge for at least 1 hour and up to overnight.

2. Make the coleslaw: Using a clean tea towel or a nut milk bag, wring any excess juice from the sauerkraut (reserve the juice and store it in the fridge in a jar; it makes a great gut-healing, probiotic shot). In a large bowl, mix together the sauerkraut, carrots, jalapeño, onions, orange zest and juice, olive oil, salt, and honey until well combined. Place in the fridge to let the flavors meld while you finish the chicken.

(recipe continues)

TIP: Be sure to buy your sauerkraut from the refrigerated section of the grocery store—it's the number one indicator that it's fermented (rather than just pickled) and is bursting with the live bacteria that you want to nurture your microbiome.

3. Preheat the oven to 350°F. Line a baking sheet with parchment paper.

4. Add the cornflakes to a large bowl. Use a wooden spoon to break up the flakes into smaller pieces, then mix in the almond flour, paprika, black pepper, and remaining ½ teaspoon of salt. Remove the chicken from the milk marinade, allowing any excess to drip off. Add it to the cornflake-flour mixture and turn to coat, pressing it to adhere. Arrange the chicken strips on the prepared baking sheet, spacing them apart. Bake for 30 to 45 minutes, until browned on the bottom and cooked through (cut the largest one in half to check).

5. Stir the coleslaw just before serving to redistribute the juices. Divide the chicken and coleslaw between 2 plates. Drizzle the chicken with the hot honey and serve immediately.

Hot Honey

Makes 1 cup

1 cup honey

2 hot chilies (Fresno, habanero, or Thai), chopped

Combine the honey and chilies in a small pot. Bring to a simmer over medium-low heat, then reduce the heat to very low and cook for 1 hour to infuse. Remove the pan from the heat and taste; add more honey or more chilies as needed. Let cool for 30 minutes, then strain through a fine-mesh sieve or cheesecloth into a glass jar. Store in the fridge for up to a month.

Crispy Orange Chicken with Lemon-Ginger Broccoli Rice

Serves 2

FOR THE CHICKEN

½ cup vegetable broth

Grated zest and juice of 1 orange

1 tablespoon rice vinegar

2 tablespoons coconut sugar

1 teaspoon peeled, minced ginger

2 garlic cloves, minced

2 tablespoons tamari or soy sauce

1 tablespoon toasted sesame oil

4 teaspoons arrowroot powder, plus ⅓ cup for coating chicken

1 large egg, beaten

½ cup coconut oil

2 boneless, skinless, chicken breasts (about 1 pound), cut into 1-inch pieces

White sesame seeds, to garnish

2 green onions, white and light green parts only, thinly sliced, to garnish

Red chilies, seeded and chopped, to garnish

TIP: While riced vegetables are increasingly available to purchase in grocery stores, you can easily make your own from any cruciferous vegetable. Simply wash and dry it well, trim any woody ends, and roughly chop it (stems and all). Pulse in a food processor until it reaches a rice-like texture.

When I was in high school, my friends and I would spend hours at the local Panda Express. We flirted with boys, complained about our parents, and did our homework, all while eating the Chinese food chain's infamous orange chicken. This version of the dish provides a far more adult-friendly center to gather around, although it still has the crunchy bite and that sticky, sweet orange syrup that makes the fast-food version so cravable—but this one utilizes real orange juice (gasp!) and the zippy zest (double gasp!), so it tastes even better. Paired with bright-green, super-fresh lemon-ginger broccoli rice, it'll leave your gut happy and you feeling energetic, not weighed down. I love doubling or even tripling this one to wow a crowd. If you're prepping it with a partner, have one of you make the chicken while the other handles the broccoli rice.

1. Make the chicken: Combine the vegetable broth, orange zest and juice, rice vinegar, coconut sugar, ginger, garlic, tamari, and toasted sesame oil in a small saucepan. Bring to a boil over medium heat. Reduce the heat to low and simmer the sauce until it's reduced by one-quarter, about 5 minutes. Add the 4 teaspoons of arrowroot powder, a little bit at a time, whisking until the sauce thickens. Remove the pan from the heat.

2. Set up a frying station next to the stove with the beaten egg in one wide, shallow bowl and the ⅓ cup of arrowroot powder in a separate wide, shallow bowl. Melt the coconut oil in a medium skillet over medium-high heat. Dip the chicken in the egg, allowing any excess to drip off, then into the arrowroot, turning to coat and pressing to adhere. Add the chicken to the pan, working in batches to avoid overcrowding, and cook for 4 to 5 minutes per side, until deep golden brown all over. Transfer to a paper towel-lined plate to drain.

FOR THE BROCCOLI RICE

1 tablespoon coconut oil

2 garlic cloves, minced

1 teaspoon peeled, minced ginger

3 cups broccoli rice (purchased or from about 1 head of broccoli, see Tip)

½ teaspoon fine-grain sea salt

Grated zest and juice of 1 lemon

3. Meanwhile, **make the broccoli rice:** Melt the coconut oil in a large skillet with low sides over medium heat. Add the garlic and ginger, and cook for 1 to 2 minutes, until very fragrant. Add the broccoli rice and salt, and cook, stirring occasionally, for 5 to 6 minutes, until the broccoli is softened. Remove the pan from the heat and stir in the lemon zest and juice. Taste and add more salt as needed.

4. Wipe out the pan, then add the fried chicken and the orange sauce, and toss to coat and warm through. Serve immediately over the broccoli rice, topped with sesame seeds, green onions, and red chilies.

Ginger-Basil Bone Broth Ramen

Serves 2

Fine-grain sea salt, plus more to taste

2 bundles (about 6 ounces) uncooked soba noodles

½ cup packed fresh basil leaves

1 (13.5-ounce) can full-fat coconut milk

1 cup pastured chicken bone broth or vegetable broth

4 garlic cloves, minced

3 tablespoons Thai green curry paste

1 teaspoon peeled, minced ginger

1 cup sliced shiitake mushrooms

2 cups torn tatsoi, kale, or chard leaves

Juice of 1 lime

4 green onions, white and light green parts only, roughly chopped

Sriracha, to serve

TIP: The bone broth that comes in Tetra Paks is essentially flavored water. In order to get all the gelatin and minerals (which is where the gut-soothing benefits live), you want to buy bone broth directly from a butcher, or the kind found in the freezer section.

If ramen and green Thai curry had a super-healthy baby, it would be this soup. You could also call it fifty shades of green, with the basil-coconut milk base, green curry paste, lime, green onions, and tatsoi leaves (okay, five shades of green, but that's still a lot!). I love how flavorful this dish is, and how little prep work is involved (if you use a Microplane for the ginger and garlic, you don't even have to dirty a cutting board). Bone broth is cited by many doctors as their number one healing food—it helps soothe the digestive system, quells inflammation, boosts the immune system, and helps hair, skin, and nails stay strong and healthy. If you buy bone broth, make sure it's of a good quality (see Tip), but if you can't find it or would prefer to make your ramen vegan, veggie broth works just as well! This is an easy one-pot dish, but if you want to divide up the labor, one partner can prep the veggies, then take a break while the other finishes the ramen!

1. Bring a medium pot of water to a boil over high heat. Add a small palmful of salt, then add the soba noodles. Cook until just al dente, about 30 seconds less than package instructions, then drain and rinse well.

2. Meanwhile, set aside a few nice-looking basil leaves for garnish. Add the remaining basil leaves to a blender with the coconut milk and blend on high until very smooth.

3. In a large pot, bring the broth to a boil over medium-high heat. Reduce the heat to medium-low and add the garlic, curry paste, ginger, mushrooms, tatsoi leaves, and basil-coconut milk. Cover and let simmer for 3 minutes, or until the leaves have wilted and the mushrooms are just soft.

4. Remove the pot from the heat and add the lime juice and cooked soba noodles, then taste and add more salt as needed. Divide the ramen between 2 bowls and garnish with green onions and the reserved basil leaves, plus sriracha, if desired.

Feeling Virtuous

While everything in this book is technically healthy, this is the super-cleanse chapter, filled with recipes for when you either want to do a real detox (see the Healthier Together 21-Day Cleanup, page 000) or just feel like you want to flood your system with nutrients. Perhaps you've been under the weather or you've been indulging a lot recently. It's amazing how quickly one delicious, vegetable-packed meal can reset your taste buds and remind you of how good your body and mind can look and feel. There's a special emphasis on detoxifying ingredients in this section, and there's no meat to be found: while I'm not opposed to meat in general (see page 12), it is a bit more taxing on your digestive system, and these recipes were designed to give your system a bit of a break.

Actually Delicious Green Detox Soup with Toasted Hemp Gremolata

Serves 2

3 tablespoons high-heat oil

1 medium yellow onion, roughly chopped

1 fennel bulb, roughly chopped (fronds reserved)

½ teaspoon fine-grain sea salt

2 cups chopped kale leaves

2 cups vegetable broth

1 garlic head, minced

⅓ cup hulled hemp seeds

Grated zest and juice of 1 lemon

¼ cup loosely packed fresh cilantro

¼ cup loosely packed fresh flat-leaf parsley

Freshly ground black pepper, to serve (optional)

If you hate detox soups, I can't say I blame you—their drab flavor and the searing hunger pangs they induce don't exactly scream desirable. This is a detox soup, yes, but it's also satisfying, with savory sautéed onion and fennel, and a bright lemon note. It also packs in more vegetables than most people eat in a week, each with a plethora of health benefits (fennel soothes the gut, kale supports the blood and liver, and garlic is super-antibacterial). The hemp gremolata adds a delightfully crunchy texture and complete protein to the dish, meaning that, unlike most detox soups, this one is filling, for real. If you're cooking this with a partner, one of you can chop the garlic and prepare the gremolata while the other makes the soup.

1. **Make the soup:** Heat 2 tablespoons of oil in a large pot over medium-high heat. When it shimmers, add the onions, chopped fennel bulb, and ¼ teaspoon of salt, and cook, stirring occasionally, until the onions just begin to brown, 3 to 5 minutes. Stir in the kale and cook, stirring occasionally, until it wilts, 3 to 4 minutes. If any browned bits stick to the bottom of the pot while cooking, add 1 tablespoon water at a time to loosen them up. Pour in the vegetable broth and bring to a boil, then reduce the heat to low and cover. Simmer, covered, for 10 minutes. Remove the pot from the heat.

2. Immediately stir in two-thirds of the minced garlic, then let the soup cool, uncovered, for about 10 minutes.

3. Meanwhile, **make the gremolata:** Heat the remaining 1 tablespoon of oil in a medium skillet over medium heat. When it shimmers, stir in the hemp seeds, remaining ¼ teaspoon of salt, and remaining garlic. Spread the mixture into a single layer in the bottom of the pan, then cook, stirring and redistributing into a single layer occasionally, until the hemp and garlic are golden brown and fragrant, about 3 minutes. Transfer to a medium bowl. Chop the fennel fronds. Let cool for a few minutes, then stir in the lemon zest and fennel fronds.

4. Add the cilantro, parsley, and lemon juice to the soup. Transfer the soup to a blender, or use an immersion blender in the pot, and blend until very smooth.

5. Ladle the soup into 2 bowls and top with a generous amount of the gremolata. Garnish with pepper, if desired.

Moroccan-ish Sunset Salad

Serves 2

⅓ cup uncooked black beluga lentils or French green lentils, rinsed

2 medium carrots

1 medium raw beet, peeled

½ cup fresh flat-leaf parsley, stems removed and chopped

⅓ cup roughly chopped pitted dates (Medjool or Deglet Noor)

½ cup roughly chopped raw, shelled pistachios

¼ teaspoon ground cumin

½ teaspoon ground cinnamon

¼ teaspoon paprika

1 garlic clove, minced

2 tablespoons olive oil

Juice of ½ lemon

½ teaspoon fine-grain sea salt

TIP: If desired, to increase the digestibility of the lentils and the speed of cooking, put them in a large bowl and cover them with warm water before making this recipe. Add a splash of raw apple cider vinegar and a dash of sea salt, and let them sit, loosely covered with plastic wrap, at room temperature for 12 to 24 hours. Then drain, rinse, and prepare as instructed, cutting the cooking time roughly in half.

If you're a beet hater, I challenge you to try them grated: grated vegetables taste sweeter than whole ones because the action of grating breaks down their cell walls and exposes more of their flavor. (If you still hate 'em, fine—just sub more carrots here and miss out on the sunset color palette.) In this salad, I take advantage of that sweetness with a riff on the French classic carrot salad, adding traditional Moroccan spices like cumin and cinnamon, and texture from the meaty pistachios and chewy, sweet dates. The black lentils lend a beautiful color and plant-based protein to make a hearty, satisfying meal. Doubled or tripled, this dish is a great make-ahead lunch—the longer the flavors mingle, the better they get. If you're making this with a partner, one of you can prepare the lentils while the other shreds the vegetables and tosses the salad.

1. Place the lentils in a large pot. Cover with water by a few inches, then bring to a rapid simmer over high heat. Reduce the heat to medium-low, cover, and gently simmer for 35 to 45 minutes, or until tender. Drain and rinse the lentils and transfer to a large bowl. Let cool to room temperature, about 15 minutes (you can transfer them to the fridge or freezer to expedite the process).

2. While the lentils cool down, shred the carrots using the large holes on a box grater, then do the same with the beet.

3. Add the shredded vegetables to the bowl with the lentils, along with the parsley, dates, pistachios, cumin, cinnamon, paprika, garlic, olive oil, lemon juice, and salt. Toss to combine well, then divide the mixture between 2 bowls to serve.

Sleepytime Dinner Smoothie

Serves 2

2 cups greens of choice

1 tablespoon chia seeds

2 tablespoons hulled hemp hearts

2 tablespoons unflavored collagen peptides

1 small avocado, peeled and pitted

1 banana, fresh or frozen

2 cups peeled, cubed sweet potato, steamed and cooled (from 1 medium sweet potato)

2 teaspoons ground cinnamon

¼ teaspoon ground nutmeg

¼ teaspoon ground allspice

1 teaspoon vanilla extract

Pinch of fine-grain sea salt

Ice

While you can technically make any of the smoothies on page 166 as a quick, fresh dinner, this one is specifically designed to lull you off into a great night's sleep. Sweet potatoes are often cited by doctors I work with as one of the best foods for sleep, with the perfect blend of complex carbohydrates and potassium. The addition of a hefty dose of healthy fat and protein will keep your blood sugar stable throughout the night (this is *the* secret to not waking up at 2 or 3 in the morning), and collagen has been found to encourage the release of melatonin, the sleep hormone. Plus, it takes just minutes to make and tastes like pumpkin pie. You can use any type of green you'd like: spinach has the most neutral flavor, but whatever's in season locally works great, too.

Place the greens, chia seeds, hemp hearts, collagen peptides, and 3 cups of water in a blender and blend until very smooth. Add the avocado, banana, sweet potato, cinnamon, nutmeg, allspice, vanilla, salt, and ice (if using), and blend again until very smooth.

TIP: To save time, I like to steam sweet potatoes in batches and keep them on hand in my freezer. To freeze steamed sweet potatoes, spread them out on a parchment-lined baking sheet and place in the freezer until they're frozen (4 to 5 hours), then transfer them to a plastic bag. This way they'll avoid clumping together. For this recipe, either frozen or freshly steamed sweet potato cubes work well, but don't add the ice if you're using frozen.

Sweet Potato Tostada with Refried Black Beans & Creamy Pepita Cilantro Sauce

Serves 2

FOR THE BEANS

2 tablespoons ghee or avocado oil

1 medium yellow onion, minced

½ teaspoon fine-grain sea salt, plus more to taste

3 garlic cloves, minced

¼ teaspoon ground cumin

1 (15-ounce) can black beans, drained and rinsed

⅛ teaspoon freshly ground black pepper

FOR THE SAUCE

¾ cup pepitas

¼ teaspoon fine-grain sea salt

½ cup fresh cilantro

3 garlic cloves

Grated zest and juice of 1 lime

⅛ to ¼ teaspoon chipotle powder

1 medium sweet potato, sliced lengthwise into planks

Fine-grain sea salt

This is one of my favorite virtuous dishes, mostly because it doesn't taste virtuous at all. A play on the trendy sweet potato toast, here I take sweet potato planks and pan-fry them to make a crispy "tostada" base. Topped with beans, tomato, avocado and onion, it has the ingredients of a salad, but the flavor profile of your favorite fast-food Mexican dish. The pepita-cilantro sauce is a game changer: it's garlicky, limey, and you're going to want to put it on everything (I especially recommend pairing it with the Charred Chipotle Poblano and Butternut Squash Taquitos on page 146). If you're making this with a partner, one person can handle the beans while the other makes the sauce and prepares the additional fresh toppings.

1. **Make the beans:** In a small, heavy-bottomed pot, heat 1 tablespoon of ghee over medium-high heat. When it shimmers, add the onions and salt, and sauté until the onions are translucent. Add the garlic and cumin and cook for 1 more minute, until fragrant. Add the beans and ¼ cup of water. Use a potato masher or fork to mash the beans as they cook, about 5 minutes, until they're warmed through and smooth, with some texture.

2. **Make the sauce:** Place the pepitas in a large skillet over medium heat and toast until golden brown, 3 to 5 minutes. Set aside ¼ cup of the toasted pepitas for topping, then transfer the remaining ½ cup to a blender or food processor. Add the salt, cilantro, garlic, lime zest and juice, chipotle powder, and ¾ cup of water, and blend or process until a smooth, lightly textured sauce forms.

TO SERVE

½ small beefsteak tomato, chopped into ½-inch chunks

½ small avocado, chopped into ½-inch chunks

¼ small red onion, finely chopped

3. Return the same skillet to medium-high heat and add the remaining 1 tablespoon of ghee. When it shimmers, add the sweet potato planks in a single layer, working in batches as needed. Salt the tops, then let cook until the bottoms are golden brown, about 5 minutes. Flip, salt the other side, and cook until golden brown, about 5 minutes more.

4. Divide the planks between 2 plates, then top with beans, tomatoes, avocado, red onions, the reserved pepitas, and a generous drizzle of the sauce.

Broccoli Rice Tabbouleh with Lemon & Dill

Serves 2

1 cup raw walnuts, roughly chopped

2 tablespoons avocado oil

4 cups broccoli rice (store-bought or homemade, page 101)

2 teaspoons fine-grain sea salt

2 medium English cucumbers, diced

1 medium avocado, peeled, pitted, and diced

½ cup chopped red onion

1 cup chopped fresh flat-leaf parsley

1 cup chopped fresh mint leaves

½ cup coarsely chopped fresh dill (fronds and tender stems only)

¼ cup extra-virgin olive oil

¼ cup fresh lemon juice

2 tablespoons white wine vinegar

1 teaspoon freshly ground black pepper

My dad and I spent several months traveling around the Middle East, where I became addicted to tabbouleh; the grain dish, studded with cooling mint, was the perfect refreshing antidote to scorching summer days. Here I add walnuts and avocado to make the dish more filling, and swap the traditional couscous for broccoli rice, which has a woody note that stands up beautifully to the fresh herbs. This is the perfect spa meal for days you want to feel super-clean (thanks to the liver-detoxifying mix of broccoli, parsley, and lemon; the debloating mint and cucumber; and the dill, a potent digestive aid). If you're backed up, it'll also get stuff moving, if you catch my drift. If you're making this with a partner, have one of you prep and cook the broccoli rice while the other chops the rest of the ingredients.

1. Place the walnuts in a large skillet over medium heat and toast, stirring constantly, until fragrant and lightly browned, 2 to 3 minutes. Transfer the walnuts to a small bowl.

2. Wipe out the skillet and return it to medium heat. Add the avocado oil. When it shimmers, add the broccoli rice and salt, and cook, stirring, 4 to 6 minutes, or until softened. Remove the pan from the heat and let the rice cool slightly, then transfer it to a large bowl.

3. Add the cucumber, avocado, onion, parsley, mint, dill, olive oil, lemon, vinegar, pepper, and toasted walnuts to the broccoli rice. Toss to combine well, then divide between 2 bowls and serve.

Warm Winter Vegetable Salad with Maple-Cranberry Vinaigrette

Serves 2

FOR THE VEGETABLES

1 cup (¾-inch cubes) butternut squash or sweet potato

1 medium parsnip, chopped into ¾-inch cubes

1 cup halved Brussels sprouts

2 tablespoons avocado oil

½ teaspoon fine-grain sea salt

⅓ cup roughly chopped pecans

FOR THE VINAIGRETTE

1 shallot, quartered

½ cup cranberries, fresh or frozen and thawed

½ cup extra-virgin olive oil

Grated zest and juice of 1 orange

1 teaspoon apple cider vinegar

2 tablespoons maple syrup

¼ teaspoon fine-grain sea salt

2 teaspoons grainy mustard

1 teaspoon chopped fresh thyme leaves

In this perfect cold-weather salad, my favorite winter vegetables are roasted (as they should be, to keep them delicious and to keep your home warm and toasty), then tossed in a delightful pink vinaigrette that tastes as if it came right from a rustic Vermont kitchen. Feel free to play around with the vegetables you use here; if you have a different favorite, sub it in. Because the salad is so hearty, it also keeps well for several days, and can be eaten straight from the fridge or rewarmed in a pan or the microwave. I like to put one person on vegetable duty while the other makes the vinaigrette.

1. Preheat the oven to 375°F.

2. **Make the vegetables:** On a parchment-lined baking sheet, toss together the butternut squash, parsnips, Brussels sprouts, avocado oil, and salt until the vegetables are well coated. Arrange the vegetables in a single layer, spacing them apart. Cover with foil and roast for 20 minutes, then remove the foil and roast for 20 minutes more, until the vegetables are fork-tender and beginning to brown. Sprinkle the pecans on the pan and roast for another 2 to 3 minutes, or until the pecans are golden. Remove the baking sheet from the oven and transfer everything to a large bowl.

3. Meanwhile, **make the dressing:** Place the shallot, cranberries, olive oil, orange zest and juice, apple cider vinegar, maple syrup, and salt in a blender or food processor and blend until mostly smooth with some cranberry flecks. If needed, add 1 tablespoon water at a time to thin it out. Add the mustard and thyme, and pulse until well-distributed.

4. Pour the cranberry vinaigrette over the vegetables and pecans, and toss to coat before serving.

Kombucha-Miso Massaged Kale Salad with Spicy Quinoa

Serves 2

FOR THE QUINOA

1¾ cups vegetable broth

1 cup uncooked quinoa

½ teaspoon smoked paprika

¼ teaspoon fine-grain sea salt

FOR THE VINAIGRETTE

1 tablespoon apple cider vinegar

1 tablespoon Dijon mustard

1 teaspoon honey

1 tablespoon minced shallot

2 garlic cloves, minced

2 tablespoons white miso paste

¼ cup kombucha

¼ cup extra-virgin olive oil

TO SERVE

4 cups torn curly kale leaves, stemmed

1 small red onion, sliced

This might be the ultimate gut-healing salad. The vinaigrette is made from three sources of probiotics: miso, a fermented soybean paste common in Japanese cooking; kombucha, a vinegary fermented carbonated tea; and apple cider vinegar, made from fermented apple cider. While each has unique benefits (the kombucha adds B vitamins, while the apple cider vinegar's acidic elements help stimulate digestion), together they pack an incredibly beneficial punch. While I'm not typically a huge fan of eating kale raw—it can be a bit tough on the stomach—here, it's massaged and "cooked," ceviche-style, in the acidic dressing, which helps break down the cell walls. Unlike most salads, this one will only get better when kept in the fridge (for up to five days). Pretty much any flavor kombucha will work here—experiment to change up the taste of the salad! If you're making this with a partner, one of you can cook the quinoa while the other whisks up the vinaigrette.

1. **Make the quinoa:** In a medium pot, bring the vegetable broth to a boil over medium-high heat. Add the quinoa, smoked paprika, and salt. Reduce the heat to low, cover, and simmer for 20 minutes, or until all the liquid is absorbed, then uncover and let stand for 5 minutes more. Transfer the quinoa to a medium bowl and place in the freezer to cool rapidly for at least 20 minutes.

2. Meanwhile, **make the dressing:** In a large bowl, whisk together the apple cider vinegar, mustard, honey, shallots, garlic, miso, and kombucha until well combined. Slowly drizzle in the olive oil, whisking constantly to emulsify.

3. In a large bowl, pour the dressing over the kale leaves. Using your hands, massage the dressing into the kale. Add the onion and quinoa, and toss to combine before serving.

Immune-Boosting Turmeric Golden Milk Daal

Serves 2

1 tablespoon high-heat oil

1 medium onion, minced

1 teaspoon ground turmeric

1 teaspoon ground ginger

1 teaspoon mustard powder

1 teaspoon curry powder

1 teaspoon ground cinnamon

¼ teaspoon ground cayenne

¼ teaspoon fenugreek seeds

¼ teaspoon freshly ground black pepper

1 cup dried red lentils

1½ cups vegetable broth

1 (13.5-ounce) can full-fat coconut milk

4 garlic cloves

¼ cup unsweetened dried flaked coconut

Juice of 1 lemon

¼ cup roughly chopped fresh cilantro

2 red serrano chilies, thinly sliced (optional, to garnish)

TIP: Don't sub other types of lentils here.

Part of being Healthier Together is helping each other out when you're sick, which, in my world, means making this daal at the first sign of a sniffle. It has plenty of anti-inflammatory, immune-boosting spices, like ginger, turmeric, and cinnamon, but the real secret is the garlic. When garlic is chopped and left to sit for 20 minutes, an enzymatic reaction occurs that makes it one of the most potent antiviral and antibacterial agents around (seriously—scientists are trying to figure out how to harness garlic's amazing health benefits for prescription drugs). Adding it after the daal is done cooking (but still warm) preserves its therapeutic properties, while taking the edge off its intense flavor.

1. Heat the oil in a medium pot over medium heat. When it shimmers, add the onion and cook until translucent, 3 to 5 minutes. Add the turmeric, ginger, mustard powder, curry, cinnamon, cayenne, and fenugreek, and cook for 3 minutes more, or until fragrant. Add the black pepper, lentils, vegetable broth, and coconut milk. Bring to a boil over medium-high heat, then reduce to low and simmer until the lentils are very soft and have absorbed most of the liquid, about 30 minutes.

2. While the daal is cooking, mince the garlic. Allow to sit for at least 20 minutes to allow the healing enzymes to activate.

3. Add the coconut to a dry medium skillet over low heat, and gently toast until warm and golden brown, 2 to 4 minutes. Transfer the coconut to a small bowl.

4. Remove the daal from the heat. Add the garlic and lemon juice, stirring well to incorporate. Let it cool slightly, about 5 minutes, then divide between 2 bowls and top with the cilantro, toasted coconut, and red chilies, if desired.

Roasted Cauliflower & Crispy Chickpeas with Golden Ghee Dressing

Serves 2

3 tablespoons ghee

1 small shallot, minced

2 garlic cloves, minced

¼ teaspoon ground cinnamon

½ teaspoon ground turmeric

½ teaspoon fine-grain sea salt, plus more to taste

½ small head cauliflower, cut into florets

1 (15-ounce) can chickpeas, drained and rinsed

¼ cup pepitas

1 small apple, cut into matchsticks

Juice of 1 lemon

¼ cup fresh flat-leaf parsley, finely chopped

It wouldn't be hyperbole to say that I'm obsessed with this dish. The ingredients seem like a strange combo at first (raw apple with roasted cauliflower?), but they work superwell together: the cauliflower is coated with warming, anti-inflammatory, and metabolism-boosting spices, then roasted until it's nutty, sweet, and perfect. Then it's tossed with lemon-brightened quercetin-rich apples and crunchy protein-packed chickpeas and pepitas (pumpkin seeds). It's also easy enough to make for a quick weeknight dinner.

1. Preheat the oven to 375°F. Line a baking sheet with parchment paper.

2. Heat the ghee in a small pot over medium-low heat. When it shimmers, add the shallots and cook 3 to 5 minutes, stirring occasionally, until translucent. Add the garlic, cinnamon, turmeric, and salt. Cook until fragrant, 1 to 2 minutes more, then remove the pot from the heat.

3. On the prepared baking sheet, pour the ghee mixture over the cauliflower and chickpeas and toss to coat. Arrange the cauliflower and chickpeas in a single layer, spacing them apart as much as possible. Roast for 20 to 25 minutes, or until the cauliflower is golden brown on the bottom, then flip and bake for another 20 minutes, or until more deeply golden all over. Add the pepitas and roast for 5 more minutes, until golden brown.

4. Meanwhile, place the apple matchsticks in a large bowl, along with the lemon juice, and toss to coat.

5. Add the roasted cauliflower, chickpeas, and pepitas to the bowl with the apples. Add the parsley and toss to combine. Taste and add more salt as needed. Divide between 2 bowls and serve immediately.

Cocktails
& Bar Bites

Is it just me, or is going out to bars not all that much fun? They're loud and I end up blowing far too much money on tiny, watered-down drinks. Instead of going out, why not have a Healthier Together night at someone's home? Make some small plates, shake up a few cocktails, or put out some wine. It'll be just as much fun and way cheaper, and you'll actually be able to hear each other. And before you ask: yes, alcohol can be part of a Healthier Together lifestyle—find out more about this on page 134.

Brussels Sprout & Toasted Almond Tacos

Serves 2

⅓ cup sliced raw almonds

2 tablespoons avocado oil

2 medium yellow onions, sliced

½ teaspoon fine-grain sea salt

¼ cup apple cider vinegar

2 cups shredded Brussels sprouts (see Tip)

4 (6-inch) corn tortillas

The original Empellon Taqueria in New York City's West Village is the best kind of happy hour spot—dark and sexy with addictive chips, nine types of salsa, and perfectly salted margaritas. But the real reason I go is for the best Brussels sprout tacos I've ever had, which I've taken inspiration from here. This recipe has actually prevented me from personally spending hundreds of dollars at Empellon's happy hours, and the fact that they're healthier than the original? Just an added bonus. The apple cider vinegar–caramelized onions are the secret: they take a little while to make, but it's mostly hands-off time, and the results are a perfect balance of sweetness and acidity. It's a one-skillet dish, and thus only needs one person to make it, so feel free to give your partner (or yourself!) the night off from cooking.

TIP: You can buy preshredded Brussels sprouts at many grocery stores these days, including Whole Foods and Trader Joe's. If you can't find them, use a mandoline to thinly slice them, pulse halved Brussels sprouts in a food processor fitted with the slicing disk (my favorite method), or just roughly chop them.

1. Place the almonds in a medium skillet over medium heat and toast until just golden, 3 to 5 minutes. Transfer the almonds to a plate.

2. Return the skillet to medium-high heat and add 1 tablespoon of oil. When it shimmers, add the onions and ¼ teaspoon of salt, stirring to coat. Cook for about 10 minutes, stirring occasionally, until most of the onions are browned. Reduce the heat to low and add the apple cider vinegar. Cook, stirring occasionally, until deep brown and very soft (almost jammy) in texture, about 40 minutes. Transfer the onions to the plate with the almonds.

3. Wipe out the skillet, return it to medium-high heat, and add the remaining 1 tablespoon of oil. When it shimmers, add the Brussels sprouts and remaining ¼ teaspoon of salt. Cook, stirring frequently, until the Brussels sprouts are softened and dark brown in spots, 3 to 5 minutes. Remove the pan from the heat and add back the almonds and onions, tossing to distribute the ingredients evenly. Transfer the filling back to the plate.

4. Wipe out the skillet again and return it to medium-high heat. One at a time, place the tortillas in the skillet and cook for about 30 seconds on each side, or just until softened. Divide the filling between the tortillas and serve immediately.

Cheesy Turmeric Rosemary Popcorn

Serves 2

4 tablespoons ghee

¼ cup unpopped popcorn kernels

1 tablespoon minced fresh rosemary

2 tablespoons nutritional yeast

½ teaspoon ground turmeric

½ teaspoon fine-grain sea salt

⅛ teaspoon freshly ground black pepper

Nutritional yeast is, in my humble opinion, the very best popcorn topper. The B-vitamin and protein-packed seasoning has a super-cheesy flavor (without any actual cheese!), and its flaky texture allows it to easily adhere to popcorn, getting up inside all the little crevices for intense bursts of flavor. With this quick rosemary-infused buttery ghee, it's perfect to whip up any time you want to satiate your snack cravings with something healthy and delicious. (I personally think popcorn, a fiber-filled whole grain, is one of the best snacks because it takes so long to eat, and thus allows you to munch for hours.) Make the popcorn in a pan as directed, or use an air popper or any other popping method you like. If you're cooking this with a partner, one of you can pop while the other makes the topping.

1. Melt 2 tablespoons of ghee in a large pot over medium heat. Add 3 kernels of popcorn. Once they've popped, add the remaining popcorn, stir gently to coat, cover, and remove the pot from the heat. Count to 30, then return the pot to medium-low heat. Listen to the popcorn pop, shaking the pot gently a few times, until the popping slows down to 1 pop every few seconds. Remove the pot from the heat and immediately transfer the popcorn to a large bowl.

2. Wipe out the pot and return it the stove over low heat. Add the remaining 2 tablespoons of ghee and the rosemary, and cook over low heat for 2 minutes, until fragrant. Turn off the heat and let the mixture sit for 3 more minutes to infuse the ghee with rosemary flavor, then pour it over the popcorn and toss to coat evenly. Sprinkle the nutritional yeast, turmeric, salt, and pepper over the popcorn and toss again to coat. Serve immediately.

Thyme-Tossed Carrot Fries with Blackberry Ketchup

Serves 2

FOR THE KETCHUP

1½ cups blackberries, fresh or frozen and thawed

3 tablespoons apple cider vinegar

Juice of 1 small lime

⅓ cup coconut sugar

¼ teaspoon ground ginger

¼ teaspoon fine-grain sea salt

½ teaspoon freshly ground black pepper

2 tablespoons tomato paste

2 teaspoons arrowroot powder

FOR THE FRIES

10 medium carrots

1 tablespoon arrowroot powder

¾ teaspoon fine-grain salt

2 tablespoons avocado oil

2 teaspoons fresh thyme leaves

Sure, you could eat these carrot fries with any ketchup you already have on hand, but once you start making your own, you'll be stunned at how easy it is to create something more complex and satisfying—with so much less sugar and no weird additives! This ketchup uses a blackberry base for natural blend of tartness and sweetness, a riff on the fact that, in the old days, ketchup was made from a wide variety of fruits (not just tomatoes, as it is today). The fries rely on arrowroot for a crispy exterior, which is no small feat for the frequently floppy oven fry. Feel free to use any root veggies you have on hand—sweet potatoes and parsnips work equally well. If you're cooking this with a partner, one of you can make the fries while the other preps the ketchup.

1. **Make the ketchup:** In a small saucepan over medium-high heat, bring the berries, ⅓ cup of water, the vinegar, and lime juice to a boil. Reduce the heat to low and simmer for 5 minutes, until the berries have completely burst. Using a fine-mesh strainer, strain out the seeds, then return the liquid to the pan over low heat. Whisk in the sugar, ginger, salt, pepper, and tomato paste, and simmer for 20 minutes more, or until reduced by about half. Sprinkle the arrowroot powder (don't dump it in; it'll clump) over the berry mixture and whisk vigorously. Let the mixture cook for 1 more minute, until the ketchup thickens, then remove the pan from the heat.

2. While the ketchup is reducing, **make the fries:** Preheat the oven to 450°F. Line a baking sheet with parchment paper.

3. Slice the carrots into batons by cutting them in half crosswise, then in half lengthwise, and again lengthwise, making them fairly uniform. Place the carrot slices in a

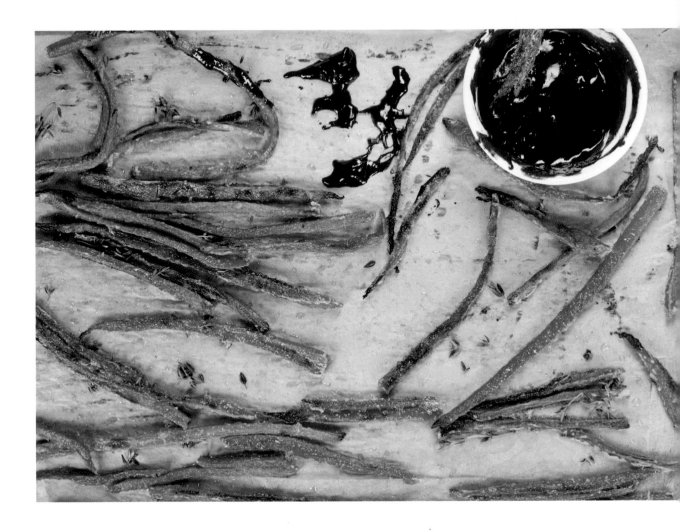

large zip-top bag, along with the arrowroot powder and salt. Seal the bag and shake so each fry is coated in a thin layer of arrowroot powder. Add the oil to the bag and shake again to coat evenly.

4. Arrange the fries on the prepared baking sheet in an even layer, spacing them apart. Bake until the bottoms are golden brown, about 10 minutes. Flip and cook until golden all over, about 10 minutes more. Turn off the oven, crack the door, and let the carrots cool inside for about 10 minutes, then remove the baking sheet, add the thyme leaves, and toss to combine. Arrange the fries on a large serving plate and serve with the ketchup alongside.

How Bad for Me Is Drinking Really?

While my dad often sends me studies about resveratrol, a polyphenol that supposedly gives wine its healing properties, if you look at the science, the health benefits of alcohol aren't really verified. You'd have to drink hundreds of bottles of wine to consume an effective amount of resveratrol. And you know those 110-year-olds who attribute their longevity to meeting their friends daily for a glass of wine? Experts say it's actually due to the social element: time spent with people whose company you enjoy lowers blood pressure, reduces stress, and has all sorts of other health benefits. The alcohol is just an accompaniment.

That said, people are going to drink alcohol, and if they want to, they should. Denying yourself simple pleasures feels needlessly punishing. With that in mind, I reached out to Dr. Frank Lipman, bestselling author and founder of Eleven Eleven Wellness Center in New York City. I know for a fact that several of his more high-profile clients drink, and I was curious about what he suggests. "Although drinking alcohol is not something I ever recommend to patients, I do understand that many people enjoy having a drink, and, therefore, I try to support them in making the best decision for their body," he told me. "I prefer low-sugar alcohols, such as tequila and vodka, as they don't cause the blood sugar spike that most other hard alcohols do. And, if you're having them in a mixed drink, use only seltzer and/or fresh citrus, rather than juice or soda."

If you prefer wine, Dr. Lipman recommends dry reds and whites, which are lower in sugar, and, ideally, choosing wines that come from vineyards that follow organic practices or that are biodynamic. "This will drastically cut down on the toxins one is exposed to," he explained. If you can't find or afford organic wines or simply don't like their flavor, I learned a little trick during a sommelier course in France. France and Italy tend to have stricter standards for their wines. In America, for instance, some producers will add chemicals to the bottle to speed up ripening, to add tannins, create oaky flavors, and more. But in France and Italy, this practice is prohibited. So, if organic wine isn't an option, a French or Italian wine (even a cheap or nonorganic one) is a good substitute.

For beer, Dr. Lipman recommends going gluten-free, and sticking to beers that are lower in sugar.

My personal favorite cocktail is vodka with soda water and a few dashes of flavored bitters—I especially love grapefruit, lavender, and orange. It's hydrating and fairly clean, and the bitters promote gut health and digestion, an added bonus. Do be careful with your bitters selection though, since many brands have added artificial color. I like Scrappy's and Dram Apothecary. If you're feeling a bit fancier, try one of the recipes in this chapter, which rely on healthier ingredients for a nutritional boost with your buzz. Bottoms up!

Extra Bloody Mary

Serves 2

1 cup (1-inch pieces) peeled beet (from 1 medium beet), steamed and cooled

2 cups pure tomato juice

2 garlic cloves

Grated zest and juice of 1 lime

2 to 3 teaspoons hot sauce

¼ teaspoon celery salt

½ teaspoon tamari or soy sauce

⅓ cup vodka

Ice

2 celery stalks, to garnish

Quick-Pickled Crudités (page 145), for garnish

If you're looking for a hair of the dog, this is a cocktail that'll truly cure your hangover. With antibacterial garlic, metabolism-boosting hot sauce, and a hefty dose of beets, a potent liver and blood purifier, you'll be feeling better in no time.

1. Place the beets in a blender and add the tomato juice, garlic, lime zest and juice, hot sauce, celery salt, tamari, and vodka. Blend until smooth.

2. Serve in 2 tall glasses filled with ice, garnished with celery and pickled veggies.

Kombucha Aperol Spritz

Serves 2

2 long strips of orange peel

Ice cubes

1 cup plain or orange-flavored kombucha

½ cup Aperol

½ cup prosecco, preferably organic

An Aperol spritz is my personal favorite summer drink, and here kombucha adds a nice B-vitamin-filled, gut-friendly kick. Fun fact: Aperol is actually a digestif which means it's filled with herbs that'll ease bloat and indigestion.

Fold the orange peels in half, then wipe them around the lip and inside 2 wineglasses, before dropping one into the bottom of each. Add a few large ice cubes to each glass, then add the kombucha and Aperol, dividing evenly. Stir to combine, then top with prosecco, stir once more, and serve.

White Tea & Muddled Basil Mojito

Serves 2

6 white tea bags

2 limes

Handful of fresh mint leaves, plus sprigs to garnish

Handful of fresh basil leaves, plus sprigs to garnish

Ice cubes

2 ounces white rum

2 tablespoons honey

½ cup sparkling water

When you're craving a vegetal, fresh-from-the-garden taste, this should be your go-to. White tea and basil are both bursting with cell-protecting polyphenols, and elevate the standard mojito to something truly cravable.

1. Bring ½ cup of water to a boil in a small pot over high heat, then remove the pot from the heat. Add the tea bags, cover, and steep for 3 minutes. Discard the tea bags and let cool to room temperature.

2. Meanwhile, cut 1 lime into quarters. In each of 2 highball glasses, muddle 2 lime wedges, half the mint, and half the basil. Squeeze the juice from the remaining lime into each glass. Add a few large ice cubes, then top each with 1 ounce of rum, 1 tablespoon of honey, ¼ cup of brewed tea, and ¼ cup of sparkling water. Stir, then garnish with mint and basil sprigs and sip through a straw.

EXTRA
BLOODY
MARY

KOMBUCHA
APEROL
SPRITZ

WHITE TEA &
MUDDLED BASIL
MOJITO

Stone Fruit & Basil "Mascarpone" Bruschetta

Serves 2

¾ cup raw cashews, soaked 1 4 hours, then drained

1 teaspoon honey

½ teaspoon vanilla extract

⅛ teaspoon fine-grain sea salt

Grated zest and juice of 1 Meyer lemon

4 small pieces of sliced sourdough baguette (see page 22)

1 stone fruit (pluot, plum, apricot, peach, nectarine), pitted and sliced

A handful of fresh basil leaves, torn

Let's get this out of the way: I normally HATE fake cheese. I hate all fake food, really—I'd much rather have a high-quality version of the real thing. But . . . if you pretend I didn't call this "mascarpone," which is really just a reference point, and think of it as a creamy, tangy, zesty spread that's the perfect counterpoint to summer stone fruit, well, that's an entirely different story. During warmer months, I like to keep a big batch of this cashew cream in my fridge (it keeps for about two weeks) so I can make a quick bruschetta with whatever produce I bring home from the farmer's market. It's the best way to eat fresh fruit for dinner and call it a meal.

1. In a food processor, process the cashews, 2 tablespoons of water, the honey, vanilla, salt, and lemon zest and juice, scraping down the sides as needed, until well combined.

2. Toast the bread and spread liberally with the cashew cream. Top with stone fruit and sprinkle with basil.

Jalapeño Hush Puppies with Honey Butter

Serves 2

FOR THE HUSH PUPPIES

2 cups chopped golden beets
(3 medium beets), steamed
and cooled

1 medium egg

1 tablespoon onion powder

1 tablespoon garlic powder

2 teaspoons baking powder

½ teaspoon fine-grain sea salt

1½ cups cornmeal

½ jalapeño, seeded and minced

Ghee or avocado oil, to pan-fry

Honey butter (recipe follows)

TIP: If you prefer to bake the hush puppies, carefully roll the dough balls through a bowlful of oil, then place them on a parchment-lined baking sheet. Brush the hush puppies with a beaten egg. Bake for 15 minutes at 400°F until the tops are cracked and the bottoms are golden brown.

Hush puppies always remind me of hanging out with my uncle, who lives in Georgia, sipping sweet tea and popping the pillowy bites into my mouth one by one on balmy Southern nights. But unlike those, these hush puppies have a secret: they are hiding two full cups of golden beets. Before you skip to the next recipe, let me say that they don't taste at all like beets, but rather take on a sweet, buttery note that perfectly complements the cornmeal and bits of jalapeño. Don't substitute red beets; they won't work nearly as well, since they have an earthier, less sweet flavor than the golden beets. You can bake these and get fairly good results (see Tip), but I personally prefer pan-frying for that signature crunchy exterior. Whatever you do, top them liberally with honey butter (see page 50), otherwise known as your new addiction.

1. Place the beets in a food processor and process until smooth. Add the egg, onion powder, garlic powder, baking powder, and salt, and process until smooth. Add the cornmeal and process until a sticky dough forms. Add the jalapeño and pulse just until distributed, with some chunks visible.

2. Using your hands, roll the dough into 1½-inch balls and place them on a large plate.

3. Heat about ⅛ inch of ghee in a large skillet over medium-high heat. When it shimmers, add the hush puppies and cook until golden on all four sides, 8 to 10 minutes. Transfer the finished hush puppies to a paper towel–lined plate to drain. Serve warm, with honey butter alongside.

Honey Butter

Makes about ⅓ cup

4 tablespoons (½ stick) salted butter from grass-fed cows, at room temperature

2 tablespoons honey

In a medium bowl, mix together the butter and honey with a spoon until well combined. Store in the fridge in a tightly sealed container for up to 2 weeks.

Quick-Pickled Crudités

Makes 2 16-ounce Mason jars

¼ cup maple syrup

1 tablespoon coriander seeds

1 tablespoon fennel seeds

1 teaspoon ground turmeric

1 teaspoon ground ginger

1 teaspoon whole black peppercorns

½ teaspoon red pepper flakes

1 tablespoon fine-grain sea salt

1 cup apple cider vinegar

1 pound mixed vegetables, such as carrots, radishes, celery, and red bell peppers, cut into spears

Crudités have never done it for me. I love a good vegetable, but unless I'm physically standing in the middle of a farm savoring the just-picked goodness of a perfectly grown carrot, most veggies could use a little something-something to reach their maximum potential. Pickling is my favorite treatment, infusing them with a tangy, salty, sweet flavor and the subtle notes of various spices. Typically, you heat the vinegar when you quick-pickle, but that kills the gut-protecting bacteria. Here I use a technique that allows the apple cider vinegar to keep all its probiotic goodness, without compromising on flavor. You can serve these as a snack on their own, but I also recommend keeping a stash in your fridge to brighten up salads, soups, and tacos, or as a way to use up extra dressings and dips.

1. In a small pot, combine the maple syrup, 1 cup of water, the coriander seeds, fennel seeds, turmeric, ginger, black peppercorns, red pepper flakes, and salt. Bring to a simmer over medium heat, then cover, reduce the heat to low, and cook for 2 minutes to infuse the water with flavors. Remove the pot from the heat and let the mixture cool for about 10 minutes, then stir in the apple cider vinegar.

2. Place the vegetables in a large glass container (or two). Pour the brine over the vegetables so they're completely submerged and tightly cover with a lid. Refrigerate for at least 1 hour, or up to 2 weeks.

Charred Chipotle Poblano & Butternut Squash Taquitos

Serves 2

4 cups (½-inch cubes) butternut squash (from about 1 medium squash)

2 small red onions, chopped

¾ teaspoon fine-grain sea salt, plus more for sprinkling

½ teaspoon chipotle powder

1½ tablespoons avocado oil, plus more for coating

1 poblano pepper

6 (6-inch) corn tortillas

TIP: To make a heartier taquito, swap ¾ cup shredded rotisserie chicken (preferably pastured) for 1 cup of the butternut squash in the filling.

During my pot-smoking phase in college, my best friend and I survived on taquitos, ordering them by the dozen from our local Mexican joint. There's something so satisfying about the crisp, salty exterior and how it gives way to the savory filling. This much-healthier version uses roasted poblano peppers, sweet red onions, and creamy butternut squash. With a crunchy outside that comes via the oven rather than the deep fryer, these taste like something you could get at a bar (or eat stoned), but they'll speed up your metabolism and make your skin glow. I recommend dipping them in Creamy Pepita Cilantro Sauce (page 112).

1. Preheat the oven to 400°F. Line a baking sheet with parchment paper.

2. On the prepared baking sheet, toss the butternut squash and onions with the salt, chipotle powder, and 1½ tablespoons of avocado oil. Arrange the vegetables in a single layer, spacing them apart. Rub the poblano pepper with a bit more avocado oil and place, whole, on the baking sheet.

3. Roast until the butternut squash is very tender and the pepper is beginning to brown and blister, 35 to 45 minutes. Remove the pan from the oven and increase the oven temperature to 425°F.

4. Transfer the pepper to a large bowl. Cover tightly with foil or plastic wrap and let it sit until cool enough to handle, about 15 minutes. Use your hands to peel off the skin and discard. Chop off the top and discard the seeds. Dice the pepper and return it to the bowl. Add the butternut squash and onions, and mash with a fork until a chunky paste forms.

5. Line the baking sheet with fresh parchment paper and arrange the tortillas in a single layer. Place in the oven for 2 to 3 minutes, or until warm and flexible. Remove the pan from the oven and spoon a thin line of filling down the left third of each tortilla, then roll them up, beginning from the side with the filling, into narrow flutes. Turn them so they're seam side down on the baking sheet. Lightly brush the outsides with more avocado oil. Sprinkle the taquitos lightly with salt, and bake for 15 to 20 minutes, or until the edges are golden brown and crispy. Serve immediately.

Crispy Roasted BBQ-Chip Chickpeas

Serves 2

1 (13.5-ounce) can chickpeas

1 tablespoon avocado oil

1 tablespoon maple syrup

2 teaspoons smoked paprika

¾ teaspoon chili powder

2 teaspoons garlic powder

2 teaspoons onion powder

1 teaspoon fine-grain sea salt

Most baked crispy chickpea recipes will have you go through the incredibly boring, annoying process of removing the chickpea skins, promising crunchier results. But what if I told you it was all a waste of time? The secret to this recipe is first baking the chickpeas dry, so the moisture that oils would otherwise trap in evaporates. After that, they're coated in the best BBQ seasoning and popped back in the oven, for perfectly crispy results with minimal effort, every single time. They taste exactly like BBQ chips, except they're packed with protein instead of inflammatory oils. I'm not saying I ever make a batch of these and call it dinner—but I'm not saying I don't.

1. Preheat the oven to 375°F. Line a baking sheet with parchment paper.

2. Drain and rinse the chickpeas well and shake them dry as much as possible. Spread out the chickpeas on the prepared baking sheet, spacing them apart. Bake for 30 to 40 minutes, or until the bottoms are golden brown.

3. Remove the chickpeas from the oven, and add the oil and maple syrup. Toss to coat, then add the smoked paprika, chili powder, garlic powder, onion powder, and salt, and toss again.

4. Redistribute the chickpeas so they're spaced apart and return them to the oven for 10 minutes more, until the coating is slightly darker in color. Remove from the oven and let cool (the chickpeas will continue to crisp as they cool) before diving in. These will keep in a zip-top bag or an airtight container at room temperature for 3 to 4 days.

Brunch
Vibes

We've become a culture that's obsessed with brunch. In cities across America, people line up and wait for hours, then drink Bloody Marys and eat overpriced waffles until 4 p.m., at which point they go home and sleep until the next morning. While I love the idea of brunch, I've found that the food is often disappointing: drab and low on flavor, it seems to be meant more as a carb-heavy vehicle for sopping up alcohol than anything else. This chapter gives brunch the same attention that's more frequently lavished on dinner. These are recipes that'll tempt your taste buds and lure your friends away from the overcrowded restaurants—plus, you'll finish eating with the energy to actually enjoy the rest of your day.

Persian-Spiced Herb & Walnut Omelet

Serves 2

6 medium eggs

½ teaspoon fine-grain sea salt

½ teaspoon freshly ground black pepper

¼ teaspoon ground cinnamon

¼ teaspoon ground nutmeg

¼ teaspoon ground cardamom

¼ teaspoon ground turmeric

½ cup lightly packed spinach, chopped

½ cup lightly packed fresh cilantro, chopped

½ cup lightly packed fresh flat-leaf parsley, chopped

½ cup lightly packed fresh dill, chopped

½ cup raw walnuts, roughly chopped

2 teaspoons avocado oil

4 green onions, white and light green parts only, chopped

⅓ cup dried cranberries, chopped

Rose petals, to garnish (optional)

TIP: To bake this dish in the oven as a frittata, let the toasted walnuts cool before mixing them into the egg mixture, along with the green onions and cranberries. Pour the egg mixture into an 8-inch pie plate and bake for 20 minutes at 350°F until it's set in the center. Add the rose petals, slice, and serve.

Kookoo sabzi is a traditional Persian egg dish, more typically baked like a frittata. I first tried it at a Persian New Year's dinner in London and immediately fell in love. It's basically a tangle of greens and herbs with a bit of egg to bind it all together; the addition of anti-inflammatory, metabolism- and immune-boosting spices, like cinnamon and turmeric, makes it one of the healthiest breakfasts around. If you'd like, you can bake this as a frittata (see Tip), but I enjoy making two individual omelets. While the flavor combination here may sound strange at first (Cinnamon! Parsley! Walnuts! Rose petals!), it really works, satisfying the need for sweet, savory, fresh, and hearty all at once.

1. In a medium bowl, beat the eggs. Add the salt, pepper, cinnamon, nutmeg, cardamom, and turmeric, and beat until combined. Add the spinach, cilantro, parsley, and dill, and mix to combine.

2. Place the walnuts in a medium skillet over medium heat. Toast, stirring occasionally, until golden brown, about 3 minutes. Transfer the walnuts to a small plate.

3. Return the skillet to medium heat and add 1 teaspoon of the oil, swirling to coat the bottom of the pan. When it shimmers, pour in half the egg mixture. As the omelet cooks, use a spatula to push the cooked portion inward so the uncooked egg mixture can flow to the outer edges of the pan, distributing the herbs evenly as well. When the omelet is set, remove the pan from the heat and sprinkle one side of the omelet with half the walnuts, green onions, and cranberries. Gently fold over the other half and slide it out of the pan and onto a plate.

4. Repeat with the second omelet. Top with rose petals, if desired, and serve.

Cardamom Banana-Bread Pancakes with Candied Coffee Walnuts

Serves 2

⅔ cup unsweetened nondairy milk

4 teaspoons apple cider vinegar

½ cup raw walnuts, roughly chopped

1 cup buckwheat flour

1 teaspoon baking powder

½ teaspoon baking soda

½ teaspoon fine-grain sea salt

1 teaspoon ground cardamom

2 ripe bananas

1 medium egg

1 tablespoon vanilla extract

High-heat oil, for pan-frying

Candied Coffee Walnuts, for serving (recipe follows) (optional)

Maple syrup, for serving (optional)

Some people think buckwheat is a grain, but it's actually a naturally gluten-free seed. It has a toasty, nutty flavor that adds more depth than most flours, and it's rich in mood-boosting, neuroprotective B vitamins and minerals. The only problem? It's super-dense. Here the addition of faux buttermilk, made with vinegar-spiked nondairy milk, gives it a lift for the fluffiest pancakes you've ever tasted. They have a hint of cardamom and a double dose of banana, both in the batter and pressed (oh so beautifully!) into each pancake. While you can definitely just top these with maple syrup (and they'd be delicious!), the candied coffee walnuts add a perfect breakfast-y bittersweetness.

1. In a medium bowl, stir together the milk and apple cider vinegar. Let the mixture sit for 10 minutes.

2. Meanwhile, place the walnuts in a large skillet over medium-low heat. Toast, stirring occasionally, until golden and fragrant, about 5 minutes. Transfer the walnuts to a large bowl and let cool slightly, then add the buckwheat flour, baking powder, baking soda, salt, and cardamom, and stir to combine.

3. Mash 1 banana with a fork. Slice the other banana into thin rounds. Add the mashed banana to the milk mixture, along with the egg and vanilla, and beat until mostly smooth, with a few lumps remaining. Add the banana-milk mixture to the buckwheat flour mixture and stir with a wooden spoon until smooth.

4. Wipe out the skillet, return it to medium heat, and add just enough oil to coat the bottom. When it shimmers, working in batches, scoop the pancake batter by the heaping spoonful into the pan so each is about 3 inches across, leaving a few inches between each one. Working quickly, press 2 to 4 sliced banana rounds into the top of each pancake. Cook until each pancake is golden brown on the bottom, 2 to 3 minutes, then flip and cook 2 to 3 more minutes on the other side, until the bananas are caramelized and the pancake is golden brown all over. Repeat with the remaining pancake batter and bananas.

5. Top with Candied Coffee Walnuts or plain maple syrup.

(recipe continues)

Candied Coffee Walnuts

Makes ½ cup

½ cup walnuts, roughly chopped

¼ cup maple syrup

¼ teaspoon ground coffee

⅛ teaspoon fine-grain sea salt

Place the walnuts in a medium skillet over medium-low heat and toast until just fragrant, about 2 minutes. Add the maple syrup, ground coffee, and salt, and stir until the walnuts are well coated and the coffee grounds are well distributed. Cook for 2 to 3 more minutes, until the maple syrup has caramelized. Remove the pan from the heat and sprinkle the walnuts over the pancakes right away, or lay the walnuts out on a parchment-lined pan so they're not touching each other and let them cool for 2 to 3 hours, until hardened, before storing in an airtight container at room temperature for up to 4 days.

Full English Skillet Bake

Serves 2

2 tablespoons ghee, avocado, or extra-virgin olive oil

1 pint cherry tomatoes, halved

2 cups sliced button mushrooms

½ teaspoon fine-grain sea salt

1 medium yellow onion, chopped

2 garlic cloves, minced

¼ cup tomato paste

1 teaspoon mustard powder

¼ cup maple syrup

1 tablespoon apple cider vinegar

3 tablespoons tamari or soy sauce

1 tablespoon molasses

1 (15-ounce) can navy beans, drained and rinsed

1 sprig fresh rosemary

4 medium eggs

Fine-grain sea salt and freshly ground black pepper

¼ cup chopped fresh flat-leaf parsley, to garnish (optional)

Zack and I lived in London for several years, and moving there was a harder transition than I'd hoped. The sun set at 3:30 in the winter, and I was trying to make friends with people who lived within a few hours of everyone they'd ever known. Slowly, though, I found my British family, and I began to look forward to weekends when we'd go away to the countryside, sleeping in farmhouses and spending the morning puttering around the kitchen, drinking tea. We always made a Full English, a UK staple that's one of the heartiest, most savory breakfasts around. Here I've eliminated the bacon and blood sausage, upping the ante on umami goodness while reimagining the dish as a baked bean version of shakshuka, topped with runny-yolk eggs.

1. Heat 1 tablespoon of avocado oil in a 10-inch cast-iron skillet over medium heat. Add the tomatoes, mushrooms, and salt, and sauté, stirring occasionally, until the mushrooms are golden brown, 6 to 8 minutes. Transfer the mixture to a medium bowl.

2. Wipe out the skillet, return to medium heat, and add the remaining 1 tablespoon of avocado oil. When it shimmers, add the onions and sauté, stirring occasionally, until the onions begin to brown, about 5 minutes. Add the garlic and cook for 1 minute more, until fragrant, then add the tomato paste and cook for an additional minute until slightly darker in color. Add 1 cup of water, the mustard powder, maple syrup, apple cider vinegar, tamari, molasses, and beans, and stir to combine before tucking in the rosemary sprig. Simmer until reduced by half, about 15 minutes.

3. Remove the rosemary sprig and discard. Stir in the tomato-and-mushroom mixture. Make 4 small wells in the mixture with a spoon, then crack an egg directly into each one. Cover and cook for 7 to 10 minutes, until the whites are just set and the yolks are still slightly runny. Season with salt and pepper to taste and top with parsley, if desired. Serve immediately.

Salmon & Avocado Eggs Benedict with Turmeric-Ghee Hollandaise

Serves 2

FOR THE EGGS

2 portobello mushrooms, stems removed

1 tablespoon melted ghee or avocado oil

½ teaspoon fine-grain sea salt, plus more for the water

2 medium eggs

½ large avocado, sliced

1 ounce smoked salmon, sliced

3 to 4 fresh chives, chopped

Freshly ground black pepper

FOR THE HOLLANDAISE SAUCE

2 medium egg yolks

2 teaspoons fresh lemon juice

½ cup melted ghee

¼ teaspoon ground turmeric

¼ teaspoon fine-grain sea salt

Pinch of cayenne pepper

¼ teaspoon freshly ground black pepper

Traditional hollandaise sauce is made with a lot of butter, which I don't think is terrible for you (see box, page 50), but I don't love to use it in excess, either, since dairy can irritate the gut and cause breakouts in some people (I'm raising my hand). Here I sub in melted ghee, which is lactose-free. It's traditionally used in Ayurvedic cooking, which made me want to add turmeric, an Ayurvedic staple and one of my favorite longevity-boosting, anti-inflammatory superfoods. Turmeric's earthy taste works beautifully here and, with the smoked salmon, avocado, and some yolky eggs, it's a divinely healthy version of a typically decadent breakfast. If you're a traditionalist, feel free to serve this on English muffins or sourdough toast instead of (or in addition to!) the portobello. If you're making this with a partner, have one of you tackle the hollandaise while the other handles the mushroom prep and egg poaching.

1. Preheat the oven to 400°F. Line a baking sheet with parchment paper.

2. Brush the mushrooms on both sides with the ghee and season with the salt. Place them stem side up on the prepared baking sheet and bake, flipping once halfway through, until fork-tender, about 20 minutes. Transfer 1 to each of 2 plates, stem side up.

3. While the portobellos are baking, **make the hollandaise:** Bring a half-full small pot of water to a simmer over medium-low heat. Combine the egg yolks and lemon juice in a medium heat-proof bowl. Whisk until doubled in volume. Place the bowl on top of the pot with the simmering water; be sure the water isn't touching the bowl—you may need to pour some out. Using an

(recipe continues)

immersion blender or a whisk and a lot of arm strength, vigorously beat the eggs as you very slowly drizzle in the melted ghee; the mixture will thicken and look like a loose mayonnaise. Remove the hollandaise from the heat and whisk in the turmeric, salt, cayenne, and black pepper. If the hollandaise thickens, you can loosen it up by whisking in warm water, 1 tablespoon at a time.

4. **Poach the eggs:** Line a small plate with paper towels and have a slotted spoon ready. Fill a large pot with water and a palmful of fine-grain sea salt, and place over high heat. When it's just about to boil, with little bubbles forming on the surface, reduce the heat to low. Poach each egg for 3 to 4 minutes, until it's opaque and firm, but with a bit of jiggle. Use the slotted spoon to transfer the egg onto the paper towel–lined plate to drain.

5. To serve, arrange the avocado and salmon on top of the mushrooms. Top each with a poached egg, then drizzle generously with hollandaise sauce. Finish with chives and freshly ground pepper.

Peanut Butter & Chia Jelly French Toast

Serves 2

FOR THE FRENCH TOAST

1⅓ cups nondairy milk

2 tablespoons maple syrup

2 medium eggs

⅔ cup unsalted, no-sugar-added peanut butter (creamy or chunky)

1 teaspoon vanilla extract

¼ teaspoon fine-grain sea salt

½ teaspoon ground cinnamon

½ teaspoon ground cardamom

6 slices sourdough or healthy bread of choice (see page 22)

High-heat oil, for pan-frying

Strawberry Rose Chia Jelly, to serve (recipe follows)

This breakfast will make you feel like a kid again. I love French toast, but frankly find it a bit boring, and, like many brunch dishes, exceptionally carb-heavy, which can mess with your blood sugar and hormones. This version stabilizes your blood sugar with protein-packed nut butter and healthy fat-filled chia seeds. The cinnamon and cardamom elevate the flavor into the adult realm, as does the optional rose water in the chia jelly. Speaking of which: once you make chia jelly, you'll never go back to the sugar-filled store-bought version. Simple, refined sugar-free, and packed with healthy fat, chia jelly is ideal for so many dishes—I always keep a stash in the fridge to dollop on oatmeal and spread on toast. While this recipe makes the perfect amount to top two servings of French toast, I highly recommend doubling it so you have some on hand throughout the week. If you're making this with a partner, one of you can prep the chia jelly while the other makes the French toast.

1. **Make the French toast:** Using a blender, blend together the milk, maple syrup, eggs, peanut butter, vanilla, fine-grain sea salt, cinnamon, and cardamom until very smooth. (If you don't have a blender, use a medium bowl and whisk vigorously). Arrange the bread in the bottom of a 9 × 13-inch baking dish and pour the batter on top. Flip over the pieces of bread, allowing them to soak up as much batter as possible. Let sit for at least 10 minutes at room temperature, or up to an hour in the refrigerator.

(recipe continues)

2. Heat enough oil to just coat the bottom of a large skillet over medium heat until it shimmers. Working in batches as needed, use tongs to place the soaked bread in the skillet in a single layer. Cook until golden brown on the bottom, 2 to 3 minutes, then flip and cook on the other side for 2 to 3 minutes more, until golden brown all over. Repeat with the remaining toast, and divide between 2 plates. Top immediately with a generous amount of chia jelly (or keep warm in the oven at 200°F until ready to serve).

Strawberry Rose Chia Jelly

Makes about ¾ cup

2 cups frozen strawberries

2 teaspoons fresh lemon juice

1 teaspoon vanilla extract

1 teaspoon rose water (optional)

2 teaspoons maple syrup or honey

Generous pinch of fine-grain sea salt

1 tablespoon chia seeds

In a small saucepan over low heat, cook the frozen strawberries for 10 to 15 minutes, stirring and breaking them up with a spoon, until they are defrosted and their juices have released, turning into a liquidy mixture. Remove the pan from the heat and stir in the lemon juice, vanilla, rose water (if using), maple syrup, and sea salt.

Sprinkle the chia seeds over the strawberry mixture, then stir to incorporate. Let this mixture sit for 15 to 20 minutes, until it takes on a gel-like consistency. Stir once more to incorporate.

The chia jelly will keep for up to a week stored in an airtight container in the refrigerator.

An Ode to the Best Weekday Breakfast

You may have noticed there are no breakfast recipes in this book (and, no, brunch doesn't count; I'm from New York, where brunch is very much its own meal). I've always found breakfast recipes to be kind of silly, unless it's a breakfast-for-dinner situation, like the Chilaquiles on page 37 or my favorite Savory Porridge (page 27). Nobody I know has ever woken up, whipped open a cookbook, set a mise en place, and prepared a crazy meal before she or he goes to work in the morning, especially with another person—and never mind having the time to sit down and enjoy it!

That said, there's one breakfast I eat every single day, and that's a green smoothie. It takes fewer than five minutes to make, and you'll get in more vegetables before noon than most people eat in an entire day. The secret is to make your smoothie truly filling, packing it with healthy fats and protein that will keep your blood sugar stable through lunch.

Here's the base formula that serves 2:

A few generous handfuls of GREENS
+ a fresh or frozen ripe BANANA
+ a handful of other FROZEN FRUIT
+ a tablespoon or so of PROTEIN
+ a tablespoon or so of HEALTHY FAT
+ a few teaspoons of BONUS ADD-INS
+ a pinch of fine-grain SEA SALT (for minerals and flavor)
+ WATER or NUT MILK to desired texture.

Blend until very, very smooth.

GREENS*

Spinach

Mixed greens

Baby lettuce

Romaine

Arugula

*Note: I avoid using raw kale in smoothies, as it is hard on the gut and thyroid.

PROTEINS

Collagen from grass-fed cows (also a gut-healing superfood)

Hulled hemp hearts (also a fat)

Nuts/nut butters (also a fat)

Chia seeds (also a fat)

FATS

Coconut butter

Nondairy yogurt

Avocado

Coconut or almond yogurt

Full-fat coconut milk

BONUS ADD-INS

Ashwagandha (stress relief)

Cacao (longevity)

Ground spices (turmeric, cardamom, cinnamon, cayenne—all anti-inflammatory)

Matcha (stable energy)

Steamed, then frozen zucchini and cauliflower (detoxifying, fibrous to keep you full)

Citrus juice + zest (great for glowing skin)

Fresh herbs (basil, cilantro, mint—detoxifying and rich in polyphenols)

Vanilla (stress-relieving and tricks brain into perceiving "sweetness")

Flavor Variations

CHOCOLATE-COVERED STRAWBERRY = a few handfuls of spinach + 1 banana, fresh or frozen + about 1 cup of frozen strawberries + a few heaping teaspoons of raw cacao powder + 1 small avocado + a few heaping teaspoons of hulled hemp hearts + filtered water

CILANTRO PIÑA COLADA = a few handfuls of arugula + a handful of cilantro + 1 banana, fresh or frozen + about 1 cup of frozen pineapple + ½ teaspoon each ground ginger and turmeric + 2 scoops of unflavored collagen powder + coconut milk + splash of vanilla extract

CHERRY CHIA CARDAMOM = a few handfuls of mixed greens + 1 banana, fresh or frozen + about 1 cup of frozen cherries + a few heaping teaspoons of raw cacao powder + a shake of ground cardamom + a couple of heaping teaspoons of chia seeds + splash of vanilla extract + cashew milk

BLUEBERRY BASIL PISTACHIO = a few handfuls of mixed greens + 1 banana, fresh or frozen + about 1 cup of frozen blueberries + a handful of frozen steamed zucchini + a handful of fresh basil leaves + a handful of raw shelled pistachios + filtered water

ORANGE CREAMSICLE = a few handfuls of spinach + juice and grated zest of 1 orange + 1 frozen banana + a splash of vanilla extract + a few heaping teaspoons of hulled hemp hearts + 2 scoops of vanilla collagen powder + 1 small avocado + a handful of frozen cauliflower + almond milk

---

Other Quick and Easy Weekday Breakfast Options.
All of these make enough to serve 2.

Mash up a whole avocado, spread it on 4 pieces of sourdough toast, squeeze some lime juice on the mashed avocado, and add some Everything Bagel Seasoning (page 28).

Sauté any vegetable in your freezer with some ghee or avocado oil; scramble in 4 eggs with sea salt and pepper. Top with leftover pesto from the Mint and Cilantro Pesto Pasta (page 42), if you have any on hand.

Combine ⅔ cup of chia seeds and 4 cups of nondairy milk; stir in cinnamon and maple syrup to taste. Let set for an hour or so, stirring occasionally, before dividing between 2 bowls and topping with any nuts, seeds, or flaked coconut you have on hand.

Slice a sweet potato into ½-inch planks, pop them in the toaster until they're golden brown on the outside and cooked through, then top with almond butter, hulled hemp hearts, and a sprinkle of fine-grain sea salt and cinnamon.

Thanksgiving Stuffing Kale & Apricot Breakfast Strata

Serves 2

2 cups roughly torn sourdough bread or healthy bread of choice (see page 22)

4 tablespoons avocado oil

½ teaspoon fine-grain sea salt

1 medium onion, diced

½ cup chopped celery (from 1 large stalk)

½ cup chopped carrot (from 1 large carrot)

½ cup sliced almonds

½ cup diced apricots, preferably unsulfured

½ teaspoon grated orange zest

1 tablespoon fresh thyme

2 cups roughly torn curly kale leaves

4 large eggs

½ cup orange juice

1½ cups unsweetened nondairy milk

Freshly ground black pepper

This dish, perfect for the person who can't decide whether he wants something sweet or savory, is based on an apricot–Grand Marnier stuffing my aunt and I make together every Thanksgiving. The original dish is decidedly not healthy, but here it gets a makeover with the addition of eggs, which help stabilize blood sugar levels, and kale, which adds extra fiber and nutrition. Instead of the Grand Marnier, I substituted collagen-boosting orange zest, which adds bursts of juicy sweetness in every bite. While I still make the original stuffing with my aunt every Thanksgiving (even in the healthiest lifestyle, balance is important!), this recipe lets me have the best parts of the dish all year round. If you're making this with a partner, one of you can toast the bread and make the egg mixture while the other cooks up the vegetables.

1. Preheat the oven to 425°F. Line a baking sheet with parchment paper. Lightly grease an 8-inch pie plate or cast-iron skillet.

2. In a large bowl, drizzle the bread with 2 tablespoons of oil and ¼ teaspoon of sea salt. Toss to coat evenly, then spread in a single layer on the prepared baking sheet. Toast in the oven for 5 to 10 minutes, or until it just begins to brown at the edges, stirring halfway through. Remove the bread from the oven and transfer to a large bowl. Reduce the oven temperature to 350°F.

3. Heat the remaining 2 tablespoons of oil in a medium skillet over medium heat. When it shimmers, add the onions, celery, and carrots. Cook for 10 minutes, or until the onions are softened and just beginning to brown. Transfer the vegetables to the bowl with the toasted bread. Add the almonds, apricots, zest, thyme, and kale leaves, and toss until evenly combined.

4. In a medium bowl, beat the eggs until smooth. Beat in the orange juice, milk, remaining ¼ teaspoon of salt, and pepper to taste.

5. Transfer the bread mixture to the prepared pie plate, spreading it in an even layer. Pour the egg mixture on top. Cover the strata tightly with foil and bake for 20 minutes. Remove the foil and continue to bake for 20 minutes more, or until the egg is set.

6. Slice the strata into wedges and serve immediately.

Extra Crumbly Grain-Free Coffee Cake with Pecan-Cinnamon Streusel

Makes 1 loaf, serves 2–4

FOR THE CRUMBLE

1½ cups pecans or walnuts, finely chopped

½ cup almond flour

⅓ cup coconut sugar

1½ teaspoons ground cinnamon

⅛ teaspoon fine-grain sea salt

3 tablespoons avocado oil

FOR THE CAKE

2 cups almond flour

1 teaspoon baking powder

½ teaspoon baking soda

½ teaspoon fine-grain sea salt

¼ teaspoon ground cinnamon

4 medium eggs

⅔ cup maple syrup

¼ cup avocado oil

1 teaspoon grated lemon zest

My friend Gretchen is one of my favorite cooking partners: she has a master's degree in alternative health and is also a complete foodie, making her an ideal candidate to get Healthier Together with. When she requested an "extra crumbly" coffee cake ("We're all just in it for the crumble," she so rightly said), I was immediately on board. Perfectly moist, mouthwateringly zesty, and surprisingly light, it's loaded with cinnamon-sugar crumble—except this crumble uses low glycemic, mineral-rich coconut sugar and healthy fat and protein–laden almond flour (plus an extra dose of metabolism-boosting cinnamon). It'll keep, covered, in the fridge for a week, but I doubt it'll last you that long. (Gretchen ate the whole loaf in a day.) If you're making this with a partner, one of you can make the crumble while the other mixes the batter.

1. Preheat the oven to 350°F. Line a 9 × 5-inch loaf pan with parchment paper, leaving a bit of extra hanging over the sides.

2. **Make the crumble:** In a medium bowl, mix together the pecans, almond flour, coconut sugar, cinnamon, salt, and avocado oil until a shaggy sand forms.

3. **Make the cake:** In a large bowl, mix together the almond flour, baking powder, baking soda, salt, cinnamon, eggs, maple syrup, avocado oil, and lemon zest until smooth. Add half the batter to the loaf pan. Sprinkle with ¼ of the crumble topping, then pour in the remaining batter. Top the batter with the remaining crumble.

4. Bake for 1 hour, or until a toothpick inserted in the center comes out clean. Serve.

Carrot Cake Breakfast Cookies

Makes 12 cookies

2 tablespoons maple syrup

2 teaspoons vanilla extract

1 ripe medium banana, mashed

½ cup almond butter

2 tablespoons chia seeds

1 cup rolled oats

½ cup chopped walnuts

2 teaspoons ground cinnamon

1 teaspoon ground ginger

½ teaspoon ground nutmeg

¼ teaspoon fine-grain sea salt

1 cup shredded carrots (from 3 medium carrots)

2 Medjool dates or 3 Deglet Noor dates, pitted and minced

Cashew Cream Cheese Frosting (recipe follows) or cream cheese mixed with honey

Carrot cake always kind of seemed like a crock to me: yes, it's great that it includes vegetables and raisins, yet with a ton of sugar and refined flour alongside, all that goodness is pretty much moot. But *this* breakfast cookie is truly a health bomb, with skin-boosting chia, heart- and brain-healthy walnuts, fibrous oats, and, of course, a ton of carrots. I find the texture and flavor of these cookies superior to that of traditional carrot cake, especially when topped with the tangy, cashew-based cream cheese frosting. They're also great on the go; my dad and I always take them along to give us all-day energy when we go hiking. These keep in a tightly sealed container in the refrigerator for up to a week. If you're baking them with a partner, have one of you tackle the frosting while the other makes the cookies.

1. Preheat the oven to 325°F. Line a baking sheet with parchment paper.

2. Stir together the maple syrup, 3 tablespoons of water, the vanilla, banana, almond butter, and chia seeds. Let the mixture sit for 10 to 20 minutes, until it's thick and gelatinous.

3. In a large bowl, combine the oats, walnuts, cinnamon, ginger, nutmeg, salt, carrots, and dates. Stir the chia mixture into the oat mixture until a thick dough forms. Drop the dough by rounded spoonfuls onto the prepared baking sheet. Bake for 15 to 20 minutes, or until the edges are golden brown.

4. Let the cookies cool until they're just warm to the touch, then top with Cashew Cream Cheese Frosting before serving.

Cashew Cream Cheese Frosting

Makes about ¾ cup

¾ cup raw cashews, soaked for
1–4 hours, then drained

1 teaspoon vanilla extract

¼ cup maple syrup

1 teaspoon fresh lemon juice

¼ teaspoon sea salt

1 tablespoon melted coconut oil

In a food processor, combine the cashews, vanilla, maple syrup, lemon juice, and salt, and process for about 3 minutes, until the mixture is very smooth and reaches a buttery texture. Add the coconut oil and process until the texture is completely smooth and creamy, about 2 minutes more. Store in the fridge in a tightly sealed container for up to 5 days.

Fancy
Food

When we go to nice restaurants, whether for a work dinner, celebrating with friends or family, or on a date, we're usually looking to be wowed by an elevated experience. This chapter is all about capturing that "Oh my God, I forgot you could do that with food" feeling at home, with dishes inspired by some of the world's best chefs, but made simple enough for any home cook. While the recipes in this section are a bit more time-consuming than those in the rest of the book, they produce sophisticated results without any special culinary skills, and guarantee that you'll suddenly be the one doing the wowing (or the one being wowed!). Because of this, cooking the meals in this chapter with a partner is especially fun. I recommend pouring some wine, cranking up the tunes, and making a whole night of it!

A Risotto for Every Season

Serves 2

4 cups vegetable broth

2 tablespoons ghee

1 small onion, finely chopped

1 garlic clove, minced

¼ teaspoon fine-grain sea salt

1 cup arborio rice

The brilliance of risotto lies in its versatility, but few recipes actually play up that fact. Here I give you one base recipe, and four seasonal mix-ins to modify it. Eating with the seasons is a great, easy way to get healthier: not only do you connect more with the land on which your food is grown, but when it's local, food is cheaper and doesn't lose nutrients in transit. Consider joining a CSA or visiting a farmer's market with a Healthier Together partner, and then curling up that night with some risotto. Have one of you handle the base risotto, while the other does the seasonal mix-ins.

1. In a medium pot over medium-high heat, bring the vegetable broth to a boil, then reduce the heat to low and cover.

2. Meanwhile, in a large pot, melt the ghee over medium heat. Add the onions, garlic, and salt, and sauté until the onions are translucent, about 5 minutes. Add the rice and sauté, stirring, for 3 to 5 more minutes, until the rice is translucent at the edges. Pour in about 1 cup of the warm broth and cook, stirring occasionally, until the broth is completely absorbed, about 5 minutes. Add another cup of broth and repeat until all the broth has been used up, making sure it gets absorbed between each addition, and the risotto is al dente.

3. Stir in your desired seasonal ingredients. Divide the risotto between 2 bowls, garnish as directed, and serve.

Hearty Shallot & Mushroom

Melt 2 tablespoons of **ghee** in a large pan over medium-high heat. Add 2 minced **shallots** and cook, tossing vigorously, for 1 to 2 minutes. Add 4 cups of your favorite chopped **mushrooms**, toss to coat, then cook, stirring occasionally, until they start to release their liquid, 4 to 5 minutes. Add ¼ teaspoon of fine-grain **sea salt**, and ⅛ teaspoon of freshly ground **black pepper**, and stir as the last of the liquid is released from the mushrooms. Deglaze the pan with ¼ cup of **dry white wine** and simmer until most of the wine has evaporated. Stir into the finished risotto.

Minty Pesto with Peas & Squash Blossoms

Make a batch of the Mint and Cilantro Pesto on page 42, subbing in **basil** for the cilantro. Once the risotto is done, stir in the pesto sauce and 1 cup of thawed **frozen peas**. Chiffonade 4 **squash blossoms** and sprinkle them over the risotto before serving.

Zesty Lemon with Zucchini, Corn & Basil

In a large skillet, heat 1 tablespoon of **high-heat oil** over medium heat. When it shimmers, add 1 cup of diced **zucchini**, 1 cup of **fresh** or **frozen corn**, and ¼ teaspoon of fine-grain **sea salt**. Sauté until the zucchini is golden brown and crisp-tender, about 6 minutes. Stir the zucchini-corn mixture, the grated zest and juice of 1 **lemon**, and ½ cup of chopped **fresh basil** into the finished risotto. Garnish each bowl with a large basil leaf.

Cranberry Ginger Butternut Squash

Preheat the oven to 400°F. In a large bowl, toss 2 cups of 1-inch cubes **butternut squash** and 1 cup of **fresh cranberries** with 2 tablespoons of **honey**, 2 tablespoons of **avocado oil**, ½ teaspoon of fine-grain **sea salt**, and 1 tablespoon of minced **fresh rosemary**. Arrange in a single layer on a parchment paper–lined baking sheet and bake until the cranberries pop and the squash is fork-tender, 20 to 30 minutes. Make the risotto according to the base instructions, but add 1 tablespoon of minced, peeled **ginger** when you sauté the onions and garlic, and put a sprig of rosemary into the vegetable broth so it infuses while the broth boils, then discard it. Stir the butternut squash mixture and 1 tablespoon of grated **orange zest** into the finished risotto.

Caramelized Parsnip Steaks with Zesty Chimichurri Sauce

Serves 2

FOR THE PARSNIP STEAK

1 pound parsnips (as uniform in size as possible)

1 tablespoon avocado oil

1 teaspoon coconut sugar

½ teaspoon fine-grain sea salt

FOR THE SAUCE

1 cup loosely packed fresh flat-leaf parsley

¼ cup loosely packed fresh cilantro

5 garlic cloves

2 tablespoons fresh oregano leaves

½ cup olive oil

2 tablespoons red wine vinegar

2 tablespoons fresh lemon juice

¾ teaspoon fine-grain sea salt, plus more to taste

¼ teaspoon red pepper flakes

This parsnip steak was inspired by chef Dan Barber's at Blue Hill, which he serves with a meat-based reduction. My lighter chimichurri sauce sneakily adds a salad's worth of vegetables, but also serves as a bright counterpart to the parsnip's sweet, grounded notes. If you're making this with a partner, one of you can make the parsnip steak while the other preps the chimichurri. I like to serve it with a light, green salad (like the one on page 196) on the side.

1. Make the parsnip steaks: Preheat the oven to 350°F. Line a baking sheet with parchment paper.

2. Chop the tops off the parsnips, then square them off on 2 long sides by slicing a bit off the long edges so they lie flat. You want them to all be about the same height when laid flat, so start with the smaller ones and cut the larger ones in half lengthwise as needed.

3. On the prepared baking sheet, toss the parsnips with the oil, sugar, and salt to coat evenly. Arrange the parsnips in the center of the baking sheet so they're not touching. Lay another piece of parchment paper on top, then cover with another baking sheet. Weigh the whole thing down by placing a cast-iron pan or a brick in the center of the top pan. Bake for 1 hour, until the parsnips are browned and tender.

4. Meanwhile, **make the chimichurri sauce:** Combine the parsley, cilantro, garlic, oregano, olive oil, red wine vinegar, lemon juice, salt, and red pepper flakes in a food processor and pulse until well combined, but not completely puréed. Taste and add more salt as needed.

5. To serve, divide the parsnips between 2 plates and top generously with chimichurri.

Fresh Fish en Papillote with Seven-Veggie Quinoa

Serves 2

FOR THE QUINOA

½ cup uncooked quinoa, rinsed

2 cups vegetable broth

½ teaspoon fine-grain sea salt

1 tablespoon avocado oil

½ onion, diced

2 garlic cloves, chopped

1 tablespoon grated fresh turmeric
(or 1 teaspoon ground)

1 tablespoon peeled, minced ginger
(or 1 teaspoon ground)

1 teaspoon ground coriander

1 teaspoon ground cumin

¼ teaspoon ground allspice

¼ teaspoon ground cinnamon

¼ teaspoon cayenne pepper

1 small carrot, peeled and cut into
½-inch rounds

1 small parsnip, peeled and cut into
½-inch rounds

½ small turnip, peeled and cut into
½-inch cubes

½ sweet potato, peeled and cut into
½-inch cubes

1 (14-ounce) can diced tomatoes in
their juices

Cooking something en papillote, French for "in parchment paper," makes a simple weeknight meal feel just a little bit special. The technique is super-versatile: a small amount of liquid, plus aromatics and protein. Here it gets a Mediterranean slant and pairs with a heavily spiced Moroccan vegetable dish. Because the most important thing when cooking fish is finding fresh fish to start with, this recipe works with whatever's fresh, so let the catch of the day at your local market be your guide. You can sub out any of the root vegetables with whatever is in season, too. Try to get a really good seal on the parchment—you want it to trap the steam so the fish cooks in it—and then be sure to cut it open at the table so you feel like you're at a fancy French restaurant. If you're making this with a partner, one of you can make the quinoa and veggie toppings, and the other can make the fish.

1. Preheat the oven to 425°F.

2. **Make the quinoa:** Combine the quinoa, 1 cup of vegetable broth, and ¼ teaspoon of salt in a small saucepan over medium-high heat. Bring to a simmer, then reduce the heat to low, cover, and cook until all the broth is absorbed, about 20 minutes. Fluff with a fork, then let it sit, covered, until you're ready to top it.

3. Meanwhile, heat 1 tablespoon of avocado oil in a medium heavy-bottomed pot over medium heat. When it shimmers, add the onions and the remaining ¼ teaspoon of salt, and cook, stirring occasionally, until translucent, about 5 minutes. Add the garlic and cook until fragrant, about 1 minute more. Add the turmeric, ginger, coriander,

(recipe and ingredients continue)

1 bay leaf

½ bunch kale, stemmed and chopped
(about 1 cup)

½ cup raisins

¼ cup chopped fresh flat-leaf parsley,
plus more to garnish

FOR THE FISH

½ bulb fennel, sliced very thin
(about ⅓ cup)

¼ cup olives, chopped

¼ cup preserved lemon, chopped

1 tablespoon avocado oil

½ teaspoon fine-grain sea salt, plus
more to taste

½ pound fish of choice (see "What's the
Deal About Buying Fish?" page 183)

2 tablespoons vegetable broth

TIP: To get a really good seal on your
papillote, seal it with some egg wash.
Beat together 1 egg and a tablespoon of
water, then brush the egg wash along the
edges of the parchment as you crimp to
make them stick.

cumin, allspice, cinnamon, and cayenne pepper, and cook, stirring constantly, until the spices are very fragrant and smell toasted, 1 to 2 minutes more. Add the root vegetables, tomatoes, the remaining 1 cup of broth, and the bay leaf, and stir to combine. Bring to a simmer, then cover the pot. Cook, occasionally lifting the lid to stir, until the vegetables are fork-tender, about 20 minutes.

4. Uncover the vegetables and discard the bay leaf. Add the kale and raisins. Bring to a boil and cook, stirring constantly, until the kale softens and the liquid thickens, 5 to 7 minutes. Remove the pot from the heat and stir in the parsley.

5. While the vegetables are cooking, **make the fish:** Place the fennel, olives, preserved lemon, avocado oil, and salt in a small bowl, and mix to combine.

6. Season the fish on both sides and place it on one side of a large rectangle of parchment paper. Top the fish with the fennel mixture. Drizzle the vegetable broth on top. Fold over the other side of the parchment paper, then fold and crimp the edges to seal them tightly (see Tip). Place the packet on a baking sheet. Bake for 10 to 12 minutes, until the packet is puffed and browned around the edges.

7. Divide the quinoa between 2 plates. Top each with a generous helping of vegetables.

8. Bring the fish to the table and, using a sharp knife, cut a slice across the top of the parchment to release the steam. Pull open the parchment, cut the fish in half, and serve, alongside the quinoa.

What's the Deal with Buying Fish?

Finding a balance between eating fish that's healthy for you and healthy for the environment can be tricky. In general, wild fish is considered the healthier option, although mercury and other contaminants may be an issue in wild-caught predators like shark, tuna, and swordfish. If you do eat heavy metal–rich fishes, I recommend upping consumption of chelators, which bind with heavy metals and remove them from your body. Simply make a cilantro smoothie the next morning, or swallow a serving of supplemental chlorella with your dinner.

Fish farming has become cleaner, more responsible, and more sustainable in the past decade or so. Buying farmed fish is also quite a bit more affordable than purchasing most wild fish. However, you should always make sure that the farmed fish you're buying is native to the environment it is being farmed in (that is, don't buy Atlantic salmon raised in the Pacific Ocean, for instance).

There are a lot of great resources out there to help you make a choice when you're at the fish counter. The Seafood Watch app from Monterey Bay Aquarium is the best known, and I like fishchoice.com as well. Here are some of my go-to fish options:

WILD SALMON FROM ALASKA: Probably the best in terms of both health and sustainability (Alaska literally has sustainable fishing practices written into its state constitution!), but also the most expensive.

FARMED ARCTIC CHAR: Similar to salmon in color and flavor, but a bit less fishy-tasting. Domestic Arctic char farms have a great reputation for being clean and sustainable.

WILD ATLANTIC MACKEREL: A high-fat fish (sometimes called "oily"). It may have mercury issues, so be sure to stick to the Atlantic variety, even if others are considered the "best choice" in terms of sustainability.

WILD ALASKAN BLACK COD: While it sometimes doesn't earn the highest mark from Seafood Watch, it's still a good choice overall.

FARMED TILAPIA OR CATFISH (DOMESTIC ONLY): Less fatty in general, so you are missing out on some great fat-soluble nutrients, but these are both much more affordable than the other varieties listed here. Generally speaking, they are a good source of protein and a great option if you are using a recipe that calls for breading or frying.

FARMED RAINBOW TROUT: One of my favorites, flavor-wise. Sometimes has a higher level of contaminants, so I eat it only occasionally, but it's a sustainable choice if you want a little variety. Bonus points if you find it from a local farm that is transparent about its growing practices.

TUNA: Contains a good amount of heart healthy fats, and is a fairly healthy choice—except for its much-maligned mercury content. There are a few things you can do to help avoid consuming too much mercury. First, buy young tuna fish whenever possible, as it's had less time to consume the smaller fish that up its mercury levels (look for the words "pole," "troll," or "line-caught" to ensure that it's eco-friendly as well). Vital Choice, an on-line sustainable seafood company, is a great source for healthy tuna.

Carrot Tartare with Crispy Capers & Super-Seeded Rosemary Crackers

Serves 8

FOR THE CRACKERS

¼ cup whole flax seeds

¼ cup chia seeds

½ cup raw pumpkin seeds

1 tablespoon onion powder

1 tablespoon chopped fresh rosemary

½ teaspoon fine-grain sea salt

½ teaspoon freshly ground black pepper

FOR THE TARTARE

Fine-grain sea salt

4 cups roughly chopped carrots (from 6 medium carrots)

2 tablespoons chia seeds

½ cup peeled, minced apple (from 1 small apple; any crisp variety works, but I like Fuji and Granny Smith)

1 tablespoon apple cider vinegar

2 tablespoons avocado oil

¼ cup capers, drained, rinsed, and patted dry

2 tablespoons chopped fresh dill

1 tablespoon grainy mustard

1 shallot, minced

Olive oil, for drizzling

Daniel Humm serves an incredibly fancy version of carrot tartare at his amazing (and expensive) Manhattan restaurant, Eleven Madison Park. The carrots are ground tableside, and you're presented with, like, 20 tiny dishes of exotic mix-ins. This version isn't quite *that* fancy, but the concept stands: the carrot tartare is slightly sweet and perfectly textured, which is a great option for those who are not so sure about eating a plate of raw meat. Indeed, this recipe is vegan, but if you prefer something more traditional (plus more protein and omega-3s), omit the chia gel and instead add eight chopped anchovies and two egg yolks to the tartare after mixing in the apples. P.S.: Don't sleep on the crackers. You'll be blown away by how easy it is to make flavorful, crispy crackers at home, and likely never buy them from the store again. If you're cooking this with a partner, put one of you on cracker duty while the other takes care of the tartare.

1. **Make the crackers:** Preheat the oven to 350°F. Line a baking sheet with parchment paper.

2. Place the flax seeds, chia seeds, pumpkin seeds, onion powder, rosemary, salt, pepper, and ½ cup of water in a medium bowl, and stir to combine. Let sit for 10 minutes until the chia seeds become gelatinous, then transfer the mixture to a food processor and process until a seedy, pasty dough forms, about 1 minute.

3. Scoop the cracker dough into the center of the prepared baking sheet. Cover the dough with another piece of parchment. Use a rolling pin (or a wine bottle) to roll out the dough until it's as thin as possible without tearing.

(recipe continues)

Remove the top piece of parchment paper and place the whole large cracker in the oven, uncovered. Bake for 15 minutes, then remove the baking sheet from the oven. Use two spatulas to carefully flip the whole cracker (don't worry if it breaks; you'll be breaking it up later anyway) and return to the oven to bake for 15 minutes more, or until just beginning to brown at the edges. Break into pieces using your hands or transfer to a cutting board and cut with a knife for more precise squares. Eat as is, or, if you want them super-crispy, reduce the oven temperature to 250°F and return the crackers to the oven for another 30 minutes.

4. While the crackers are baking, **make the tartare:** Fill a medium pot halfway with water. Add a small palmful of salt. Add the carrots, bring to a boil over medium-high, and cook until just fork-tender, about 10 minutes. While the carrots are cooking, prepare a large bowl of ice water. When the carrots finish cooking, drain them and immediately transfer them to the ice bath.

5. Meanwhile, place the chia seeds in a small bowl and stir in ¼ cup of water. Let the mixture sit for at least 10 minutes, until the chia seeds become gelatinous. Place the apples in a separate small bowl. Pour in the apple cider vinegar, toss to coat the apples completely, then let the apples sit for at least 10 minutes to infuse.

6. Heat the avocado oil in a medium skillet over medium-high heat. When it shimmers, add the capers and toast, stirring occasionally, until golden brown. Transfer to a paper towel–lined plate to drain.

7. Drain the carrots, transfer to a food processor, and pulse until minced. Transfer to a medium bowl and mix in the dill, mustard, shallot, soaked chia seeds, and apple cider vinegar–infused apples.

8. To serve, press the tartare into a 1-cup measuring cup or a small ramekin until tightly packed. Place a small plate over the cup and invert. Tap the cup gently until the tartare slides out. Drizzle generously with olive oil and top with the capers. Serve with the crackers on the side.

Asparagus Soup with Forbidden Rice & Tempura Shallots

Serves 2

FOR THE RICE

½ cup black forbidden rice
(you can sub white rice, but it
won't be as pretty)

⅛ teaspoon fine-grain sea salt

FOR THE TEMPURA

¼ cup rice flour

⅛ teaspoon fine-grain sea salt

6 tablespoons seltzer or sparkling water

1 tablespoon ground flax

1 bunch asparagus

About 1 cup high-heat oil, for frying

1 shallot, sliced

FOR THE SOUP

2 tablespoons avocado or olive oil

1 medium yellow onion, chopped

½ teaspoon fine-grain sea salt

2 tablespoons rice vinegar

1 tablespoon peeled, minced ginger

1 garlic clove, minced

1 cup vegetable broth

1 tablespoon tamari or soy sauce

1 tablespoon white miso paste

Black sesame seeds, to garnish
(optional)

One of my favorite ways to get Healthier Together is to host *Chopped* night, where Zack and I square off against another pair. We're all given a few ingredients that we combine with pantry staples to make a meal designed to wow (meaning: decisively beat) the other team. Usually one team takes cocktails and entrees, and the other handles an appetizer and dessert; it makes for great hanging out at home. This recipe came from one of those nights when my friend Stacy was given asparagus, and decided to use it every which way in this recipe. Besides being visually stunning—the black rice with the bright green soup!—it's a delightful celebration of the spring vegetable, using a mix of French techniques and Asian flavors. Have one person handle the rice and soup while the other tackles the tempura.

1. **Make the rice:** Rinse the rice well and place it in a medium pot. Add ¾ cup of water and the salt, and bring to a boil over medium-high heat. Reduce the heat to low and cover. Simmer for 25 to 30 minutes, or until the water is absorbed and the rice is cooked through. Fluff with a fork.

2. Meanwhile, **make the tempura batter:** In a large bowl, whisk together the rice flour, salt, seltzer, and flax, and let the mixture sit for 10 minutes to thicken. You want it to be about the consistency of pancake batter—a bit runny, but with some viscosity. (If it's too thick, add more seltzer, 1 teaspoon at a time, until it reaches the desired texture.) Break off and discard the woody ends of the asparagus, then chop into 2- to 3-inch pieces, separating the tips from the stalks. You should have about 2½ cups of stalks and tips. Reserve the stalks for the soup, while you tempura the tips.

(recipe continues)

3. Add enough oil to a medium skillet so that it's about ¼ inch deep, and heat over medium-high heat until it sizzles when a bit of batter is dropped in. Drop the shallot slices and asparagus tips in the tempura batter to coat well, allowing any excess to drip off, then carefully lower them into the oil using a fork or a slotted spoon. Fry until golden brown, 3 to 5 minutes, then using tongs or a slotted spoon, transfer to a paper towel–lined plate to drain.

4. **Make the soup:** Heat 1 tablespoon of oil in a clean medium skillet over medium heat. When it shimmers, add the onions and ¼ teaspoon salt. Sauté, stirring occasionally, until the onions begin to turn translucent, about 5 minutes. Reduce the heat to low and add the rice vinegar. Continue to sauté until the onions just turn golden, 10 to 15 minutes more. Transfer the onions to a blender.

5. Return the skillet to medium-high heat (no need to rinse it), and add the remaining 1 tablespoon of oil. When it shimmers, add the asparagus stalks, ginger, and the remaining ¼ teaspoon sea salt. Toss to coat, and cook, stirring occasionally, until the asparagus is browned, about 5 minutes. Add the garlic and cook for 2 minutes more, until fragrant, then add the vegetable broth and tamari. Bring to a boil, then reduce the heat to medium-low and simmer until the liquid has reduced by about half. Remove the skillet from the heat and let the mixture cool slightly, then add it to blender with the onions. Add the miso and blend until very smooth.

6. To serve, divide the rice between 2 bowls, pressing it to 1 side of the bowl. Pour the soup into the other side and top the soup with the tempura shallots and asparagus. Sprinkle with black sesame seeds to garnish, if desired.

Turmeric-Tahini Whole Roasted Cauliflower with Spiced Sweet Potato Lentils

Serves 2

FOR THE CAULIFLOWER

½ cup toasted sesame oil

1 tablespoon tahini

4 garlic cloves, minced

1 tablespoon apple cider vinegar

1 tablespoon honey

½ teaspoon ground turmeric

½ teaspoon fine-grain sea salt

1 small to medium cauliflower head

¼ cup raw pistachios, chopped

FOR THE SWEET POTATO LENTILS

1 tablespoon coconut oil

1 medium yellow onion, chopped

2 cups peeled, grated sweet potatoes (from about 1 small sweet potato)

1 garlic clove, minced

2 teaspoons peeled, minced ginger

Juice of 1 lime

¾ cup red lentils

1 teaspoon fennel seeds

1 teaspoon ground coriander

½ teaspoon ground cumin

½ teaspoon ground cinnamon

When you roast a cauliflower head whole, you get two kinds of delicious: the outside turns a toasty, nutty brown, and the inside becomes sweet and creamy. Also, it looks really freakin' impressive when you carve it tableside—although all you had to do was smear the vegetable with some spices and toss it in the oven. The sauce here is one of my favorites; I use it as a perfectly bittersweet salad dressing or heaped on grain and veg bowls. On the side, the grated sweet potatoes melt into the lentils, infusing every bite with sweetness. This dish is essentially eating pounds of vegetables for dinner with some protein-packed lentils mixed in, but if you plate it real fancy (swoosh those lentils!), you'll feel like you're at the world's nicest restaurant. If you're making this with a partner, one of you can handle the cauliflower while the other takes on the lentils.

1. Make the cauliflower: Preheat the oven to 375°F.

2. In a medium bowl, whisk together the sesame oil, tahini, garlic, apple cider vinegar, honey, turmeric, and salt to combine.

3. Remove any leafy bits from the cauliflower and trim its bottom so it sits flat. Place it in pie plate, an 8 × 8-inch baking dish, or a 10-inch cast-iron skillet. Pour about ¾ of the sauce over the cauliflower, rubbing it in with your fingers so it really gets into the nooks and crannies and the cauliflower is evenly coated. Loosely tent the cauliflower with foil so that it covers the cauliflower completely without touching it, then bake for 45 minutes, until fork-tender. Remove the cauliflower from the oven, remove

(recipe and ingredients continue)

½ teaspoon ground turmeric

3 cups vegetable broth

¼ cup pomegranate seeds

¼ cup chopped fresh cilantro

the foil, and carefully flip it over, so the top is facing down. Drizzle the bottom with the remaining sauce and bake, uncovered, for another 25 minutes, until golden brown. During the last 5 minutes of baking, spread the pistachios out on a parchment-lined baking sheet and pop them into the oven with the cauliflower until they're golden brown.

4. Meanwhile, **make the sweet potato lentils:** Heat the oil in a large pot over medium-low heat. When it shimmers, add the onions and sauté until softened, about 3 minutes. Add the sweet potatoes, garlic, and ginger, and sauté for about 5 minutes, until the sweet potatoes are softened and begin sticking to the bottom of the pot a bit. Deglaze the pan with the lime juice, stirring to scrape up any browned bits from the bottom.

5. Add the lentils, fennel, coriander, cumin, cinnamon, and turmeric to the pan. Stir to coat the sweet potato, then add the broth. Increase the heat to medium-high and bring to a boil, then reduce the heat to low and simmer, stirring occasionally, until the lentils are soft and the broth is completely absorbed, about 20 minutes.

6. To serve, spoon a generous helping of lentils onto a plate, spreading it out and creating swirls with the bottom of a spoon. Carve the cauliflower tableside, slicing it into wedges with a sharp knife and placing it on top of the lentils. Top with a sprinkle of pomegranate seeds, cilantro, and toasted pistachios.

Harissa Chicken with Pistachio & Fig Cauliflower Couscous

Serves 2

FOR THE CHICKEN

2 medium, bone-in, skin-on chicken breasts (see Tip, page 195)

2 teaspoons fine-grain sea salt

½ teaspoon ground cumin

½ teaspoon ground coriander

½ teaspoon fennel seeds

2 tablespoons chili powder

2 teaspoons smoked paprika

1 teaspoon garlic powder

¼ teaspoon ground cinnamon

⅛ teaspoon ground ginger

⅛ to ¼ teaspoon cayenne pepper

1 tablespoon ghee or avocado oil

FOR THE COUSCOUS

¼ cup ghee

3 dried figs, minced

4 garlic cloves, minced

½ cup raw, shelled pistachios, roughly chopped

½ small cauliflower head, riced (see Tip, page 100), or 2 cups frozen cauliflower rice, thawed

½ teaspoon fine-grain sea salt

½ teaspoon grated lemon zest

Juice of ½ lemon

¼ cup fresh flat-leaf parsley, chopped

If you thought you had to roast a whole chicken to get crispy skin and impossibly juicy meat, prepare to be dazzled. This recipe's two-step cooking and early salting process ensures that you will get the perfect texture every time (see Tip, page 195), and the harissa-based spice rub will have you licking your fingers. And, yes, keeping the chicken skin on is not only more delicious, but also healthier, providing fats and collagen to help make your skin glow and your hair and nails grow strong. I'm also obsessed with this cauliflower "couscous"; while cauliflower has become a ubiquitous replacement for grains, it goes to the next level here with meaty pistachios and sweet, chewy figs. If you're cooking this with a partner, have one of you make the couscous while the other preps the chicken.

1. Make the chicken: Pat the chicken dry with a paper towel. Rub the salt very generously all over, then let the chicken stand for at least 15 minutes at room temperature, or up to 24 hours in the refrigerator. In a large bowl, mix together the cumin, coriander, fennel seeds, chili powder, smoked paprika, garlic powder, cinnamon, ginger, and cayenne. Add the chicken to the bowl and rub the spice blend all over to coat.

2. Preheat the oven to 425°F.

3. Heat the oil in a large ovenproof skillet over medium heat. When it shimmers, add the chicken, skin side down, and cook it without moving until the skin is crispy and dark brown, 5 to 6 minutes. Use tongs to flip the chicken, then transfer the pan to the oven. Roast for 10 to 15 minutes, or until the chicken is cooked through

(recipe continues)

TIP: Salting protein ahead of time is the key to keeping it moist. It helps the meat become and stay tender by keeping moisture bound into the protein structure (for a great, deep-dive explanation of this technique, check out *New York Times* chef Samin Nosrat's *Salt Fat Acid Heat*).

and an instant-read thermometer inserted into the thickest part reads 165°F. Remove the chicken from the oven and let it rest for about 5 minutes.

4. While the chicken cooks, make the couscous: Melt the ghee in a medium skillet over medium-low heat. Add the figs, garlic, and pistachios and cook for 2 minutes, stirring often, until very fragrant and the garlic begins to turn golden. Add the cauliflower rice and salt, and cook for 5 to 8 minutes more, stirring occasionally, until tender. Remove the pan from the heat and add the lemon zest, lemon juice, and parsley. Toss well to combine.

5. Divide the couscous between 2 plates. Top each with a chicken breast and serve.

Sweet Corn & Thyme Custard with the World's Best Simple Salad

Serves 2

FOR THE CUSTARD

High-heat oil, for greasing

1 cup canned full-fat coconut milk

1 tablespoon fresh thyme leaves, roughly chopped

1 cup corn, fresh or frozen and thawed

½ teaspoon fine-grain sea salt

Pinch of cayenne pepper (optional)

1 medium egg plus 2 medium egg yolks

FOR THE SALAD

4 cups salad greens

¼ teaspoon fine-grain sea salt

Grated zest and juice of 1 Meyer lemon (can sub regular lemon)

1 garlic clove

3 tablespoons olive oil

I love creamy custard, especially when it straddles the line between sweet and savory, which corn does beautifully. If you're making this recipe during the height of corn season, use fresh, but, if not, please use frozen corn and don't feel at all guilty about it: frozen at the peak of ripeness, it'll actually have a better taste and health benefits than a subpar fresh counterpart. Served with my favorite simple lemon salad (once you try it, you'll be addicted), it's the perfect, elegant dinner. If you're making this with a partner, have one of you whip up the salad while the other handles the custard.

1. Preheat the oven to 325°F. Lightly grease two 6-ounce ramekins.

2. Fill a pie plate or a small casserole dish (big enough to fit both ramekins) with about 1 inch of water (it should come halfway up the sides of the ramekins when they're placed in the dish, and place it in the oven to warm.

3. In a medium saucepan, bring the coconut milk, thyme, corn, salt, and cayenne, if using, to a simmer over medium-high heat. Transfer the mixture to a blender and blend until creamy and smooth. (You can also use an immersion blender.)

4. In a large bowl, whisk together the egg and egg yolks. Whisk in a few large spoonfuls of the corn mixture, just until incorporated. Repeat, adding a bit of the corn mixture to the eggs and whisking to combine, until all the corn mixture has been incorporated. Divide the mixture evenly between the greased ramekins.

5. Carefully place the ramekins in the dish and bake for 30 to 35 minutes, until set. Let cool for about 10 minutes.

6. Meanwhile, **make the salad:** In a large bowl, toss the greens with the salt. Add the lemon zest and garlic clove, and toss to combine, massaging with your fingers so the garlic is evenly distributed. Toss in the lemon juice, evenly coating the greens with it, then drizzle the olive oil down the sides of the bowl, before tossing so the greens are evenly coated.

7. To serve, divide the salad between 2 plates, putting it off to one side. On the other side, either place the custard still in the ramekin, or unmold them onto the plates.

Deconstructed Chai Steak Salad with Coconut Smashed Potatoes

Serves 2

FOR THE STEAK

½ teaspoon ground cardamom

½ teaspoon ground allspice

1 teaspoon ground cinnamon

¼ teaspoon freshly ground black pepper

¼ teaspoon ground cloves

1½ teaspoons ground ginger

1 teaspoon fine-grain sea salt

8-ounce skirt steak, ½ to ¾ inch thick

1 tablespoon coconut oil

FOR THE POTATOES

½ pound new potatoes, preferably multi-colored (about 10 small potatoes)

1 (13.5-ounce) can full-fat coconut milk

¾ teaspoon fine-grain sea salt, plus more for the potatoes

3 to 4 teaspoons coconut oil, melted

1 tablespoon unsweetened coconut flakes

Tea is an unsung hero of the culinary world, boasting a delicate, delicious flavor and tons of antioxidants and other longevity-promoting health benefits. This riff on steak and potatoes takes the traditional flavors of chai (which simply means "tea" in Hindi, but colloquially refers to the spicy, milky drink you're probably imagining) and divides them into their component parts: the spices end up rubbed on the steak, while the black tea becomes the base of a vinaigrette to toss with peppery greens, and creamy, sweet coconut milk–smashed potatoes as a counterpoint. If you're making this with a partner, put one of you on steak and potato duty, while the other whips up the vinaigrette.

1. **Make the steak:** Mix together the cardamom, allspice, cinnamon, black pepper, cloves, ginger, and salt in a large bowl. Add the steak and turn to coat, pressing the spice mixture to adhere. Loosely cover the bowl with plastic wrap and marinate the steak in the refrigerator for at least 2 hours and up to 24 (the longer the better—see Tip, page 195).

2. About 30 minutes before you plan to cook the steak, **make the potatoes:** Place the potatoes in a small pot, pour in the coconut milk, and add just enough water to ensure they're covered. Add a small palmful of fine-grain sea salt and bring to a boil over medium-high heat, then reduce the heat to low. Cover and simmer until the potatoes are fork-tender, 8 to 10 minutes. Drain (but do not rinse) and let them sit for about 10 minutes, until they're cool enough to handle.

3. While the potatoes are cooling, preheat the oven to 425°F. Line a baking sheet with parchment paper.

(recipe and ingredients continue)

4 black tea bags (or 4 teaspoons loose leaf)

1 tablespoon honey

1 tablespoon champagne vinegar or white wine vinegar

1 garlic clove, minced

1 tablespoon minced shallot

¼ teaspoon fine-grain sea salt

¼ teaspoon freshly ground black pepper

¼ cup avocado oil

TO SERVE

2 cups arugula

⅛ teaspoon fine-grain sea salt

Drizzle the baking sheet with 1 teaspoon of oil, and use your fingers or a brush to spread a thin layer over the surface of the pan.

4. Add the potatoes to the pan, and use the palm of your hand or the bottom of a cup to gently crush the potatoes; you don't want them to break apart, but you want them to spread out.

5. Drizzle the remaining 3 teaspoons of coconut oil over the potatoes and use your hands or a brush to gently coat them. Sprinkle with salt and bake the potatoes for 15 minutes, until golden brown on the bottom; flip and bake for 15 minutes more, until golden brown on both sides. Meanwhile, put the coconut flakes in a small plastic bag and use a rolling pin or a wine bottle to crush them. When there are 2 to 3 minutes left on the potatoes, sprinkle the coconut over them and continue to bake until the coconut becomes golden brown (watch closely to make sure it doesn't burn).

6. While the potatoes are roasting, **make the vinaigrette:** In a small pot, bring ⅓ cup of water to a boil over high heat. Remove the pan from the heat and add the tea bags. Steep for 3 minutes, then remove the bags, squeezing all the liquid out of them. Whisk in the honey, vinegar, garlic, shallots, salt, and pepper. Slowly drizzle in the avocado oil, whisking vigorously to emulsify.

7. Sear the steak: Heat the coconut oil in an 8-inch cast-iron skillet over medium heat. When it shimmers, add the steak and sear for about 4 minutes per side, until browned, for medium doneness (add or subtract 1 minute to cook to your preference). Transfer the steak to a plate and tent loosely. Let it rest for about 5 minutes.

8. Make the salad: In a large bowl, toss the arugula with the salt. Drizzle the vinaigrette down the side of the bowl and toss to lightly coat.

9. Divide the dressed greens and potatoes between 2 plates, then slice the steak against the grain and serve over the greens.

Burst Cherry Tomato Linguine

Serves 2

2 garlic heads

5 tablespoons olive oil

2 pints cherry tomatoes, stemmed

1 teaspoon fine-grain sea salt, plus more for the pasta water

1 tablespoon dried herbes de Provence or dried thyme

⅓ cup fresh basil leaves

½ pound ancient-grain or gluten-free linguine

Freshly ground black pepper, to serve

When we were in Provence together one summer, Zack started roasting cherry tomatoes for breakfast and topping them with herbes de Provence from the local market and, oh my gosh, I've never eaten anything so divine. When roasted, cherry tomatoes become little balls of umami, like a cross between a normal tomato and a sun-dried one. Here they're roasted and then blended into the best tomato sauce you've ever had. The result is incredibly complex and faintly sweet, and tastes like it takes way longer (and way more ingredients!) to make than it actually does. Cooking tomatoes also ups their levels of lycopene, one of the most powerful antioxidants in the world (it helps prevent cancer, fight yeast infections, improve brain health, and more). This dish comes together easily, so have one partner kick back and get started on drinking the wine.

1. Preheat the oven to 375°F. Line a baking sheet with parchment paper.

2. Break the garlic heads apart into cloves, leaving the skin on. On the prepared baking sheet, toss the cherry tomatoes and garlic cloves with 2 tablespoons of oil, the salt, and the herbes de Provence until well-coated. Spread everything out evenly, so nothing is touching. Bake for 40 to 50 minutes, or until the tomatoes burst and release their juices and the garlic can be squeezed gently. Remove the pan from the oven and let everything cool slightly.

3. Add half the basil to a blender, along with three-quarters of the roasted cherry tomatoes and 3 tablespoons of olive oil. Squeeze the roasted garlic from its skin; add as much of the soft inside as possible to the blender before

(recipe continues)

discarding the papery skin. Blend until creamy. Taste and add salt as needed.

4. Meanwhile, bring a large pot of water to a boil over medium-high heat. Add a generous palmful of salt. Add the pasta and cook until al dente according to the package instructions. Reserve ¼ cup of the pasta water, then drain. Return the pasta to the pot over low heat. Add the cherry tomato sauce and toss to combine. Add the reserved pasta cooking water, 1 tablespoon at a time, until your desired consistency is reached.

5. Halve the reserved cherry tomatoes. Chiffonade the remaining basil. Toss both into the pasta along with the remaining peeled, roasted garlic. Top with black pepper to serve.

Coffee Hawaij–Crusted Lamb with Roasted & Pickled Onions & Fennel

Serves 2

FOR THE ONIONS AND FENNEL

1 fennel bulb, thinly sliced (reserving leafy fronds and roughly chopping them to make 1 tablespoon)

1 medium red onion, halved and sliced into half-moons

1 tablespoon avocado or olive oil

½ teaspoon fine-grain sea salt

1 teaspoon whole black peppercorns

1 tablespoon fennel seeds

1 tablespoon maple syrup

½ cup apple cider vinegar

FOR THE LAMB

1 tablespoon ground coriander

1 tablespoon ground ginger

1 tablespoon fennel seeds

½ teaspoon ground cloves

½ teaspoon ground cinnamon

2 tablespoons ground coffee

1 teaspoon fine-grain salt

1 teaspoon freshly ground black pepper

½ rack (about 1 pound) of lamb, frenched

1 teaspoon avocado oil

There are two types of Hawaij, a Yemeni spice blend—one meant for spicing coffee and one meant for savory cooking. Here I take the coffee variety, made with ginger, cinnamon, and fennel seeds, and combine it with actual coffee to make one of the best lamb rubs I've ever tasted. The side salad takes just two primary ingredients and uses them in a multitude of ways to add incredible layers of flavor: red onions are pickled and roasted with a fennel bulb, then tossed with bright-green fennel fronds. The result is sweet and tangy, comforting and fresh, and utterly addictive (even if you don't love lamb, I encourage you to try this salad). If you're making this with a partner, stick one of you on pickling and lamb duty while the other preps the vegetables and handles the roasting.

1. About 30 minutes before you're ready to cook, take the lamb out of the fridge. Let it sit at room temperature while you prep the vegetables.

2. Make the fennel and onion salad: Preheat the oven to 425°F. Line a baking sheet with parchment paper.

3. On the prepared baking sheet, toss the fennel slices with two-thirds of the onion slices, the oil, and salt to coat. Arrange in a single layer. Set aside.

4. Bring to a boil in a small pot over high heat ½ cup of water, the peppercorns, fennel seeds, and maple syrup.

(recipe continues)

Turn off the heat and let the mixture cool for 5 minutes. Place the remaining sliced onions in a small bowl or a 16-ounce glass jar and pour in the apple cider vinegar. Add the cooled spiced water. Let the mixture sit until you're ready to serve, at least 20 minutes (or up to 1 month in the fridge).

5. **Make the lamb:** Mix together the coriander, ginger, fennel seeds, cloves, cinnamon, coffee, salt, and pepper in a large bowl. Pat the lamb dry. Rub the avocado oil all over the lamb to coat completely, then add the lamb to the spices, turning to coat and pressing to adhere. Let sit for another 15 minutes at room temperature.

6. Meanwhile, begin roasting the vegetables in the preheated oven. After 15 minutes, place the lamb on a separate baking sheet and place it in the oven. When the vegetables are golden brown at the edges and the lamb reaches 145°F on a meat thermometer, about 15 minutes later, remove both from the oven.

7. Drain the pickled onions and toss them with the roasted vegetables and reserved fennel fronds. Divide the salad between 2 plates. Let the lamb rest for 5 minutes before cutting it apart into individual lollipops and serving over the salad.

TIP: What the heck is frenching lamb? Frenched lamb simply means removing the meat from the rib. You can ask for this in almost any butcher shop—it simply makes for a nicer appearance, and it's easier to cut apart the Hawaij-crusted lamb chops later. If you can't find frenched lamb, using a normal rack of lamb is totally fine!

Sweet Treats

While I've tried to give up sugar time and again, making pacts with a number of my friends, the truth is, forgoing sweet pleasures isn't really Healthier Together. When we deny ourselves life's little treats, it's easy to find ourselves resenting our healthy diets—and enjoying life a whole lot less. Instead, I recommend replacing unhealthy cravings with (often even tastier) healthy, homemade versions. While the recipes in this chapter are still undoubtedly dessert, they're all free from refined sugar, and have a good amount of protein and healthy fat to keep blood sugar levels stable. They also contain therapeutic ingredients that bring them into the more healing realm, like anxiety-reducing CBD, or cannabidiol; ashwagandha; and gut-healing gelatin. Now, instead of giving up sugar with friends, I have them over to make Healthier Together brownies or cookies—which is arguably psychologically healthier, and definitely way more fun. I also love keeping a stash of healthy sweets on hand (the Fun-Size Chocolate Nougat Candy Bars are *always* in my freezer) so I don't succumb to less healthy versions when my sweet tooth strikes.

The Best Healthy Chocolate Chip Cookie

Makes 6–8 cookies

1 large egg

1 teaspoon vanilla extract

½ cup unsalted creamy almond butter

¼ cup almond flour

¼ teaspoon fine-grain sea salt

½ cup coconut sugar

½ teaspoon baking soda

¼ cup chopped walnuts

¼ cup rolled oats

¼ cup dark chocolate chips or chopped dark chocolate

TIP: When I'm looking for healthy, organic chocolate that's sweetened with only coconut sugar, Hu Kitchen and Eating Evolved (for bars) and Santa Barbara Chocolate (for chips) are my go-tos. You can order all of them online!

Sometimes you think you want a creative twist on a cookie (pretzel, potato chip, butterscotch, coffee!), but, ultimately, nothing beats the classic: a perfect, grain-free chocolate chip cookie. These babies have everything you want: the crispy edge that cedes to a chewy center; a rich, buttery flavor; studs of walnuts, oats, and chocolate chips—yet they're completely grain-free and refined sugar-free, packed with protein, and won't spike and crash your blood sugar as a normal cookie would. (Zack uses this as an excuse to eat them for breakfast, but you do you. . . .)

1. Preheat the oven to 375°F. Line a baking sheet with parchment paper.

2. In a large bowl, beat together with a large spoon the egg, vanilla, and almond butter until combined. Stir in the almond flour, salt, coconut sugar, and baking soda until smooth. Stir in the walnuts, oats, and chocolate chips, working the dough a bit to get everything distributed evenly (the dough will be thick—that's okay).

3. Scoop the dough into rounded teaspoonfuls and drop them onto the prepared baking sheet. Bake for 10 to 15 minutes, until the edges turn golden brown.

4. Remove the cookies from the oven and let them cool on the pan for 10 minutes before transferring them to a wire rack to cool completely. While the texture of these is best on the first day (I like to make small batches and eat them fresh), they'll keep uncovered at room temperature for 2 to 3 days.

Chocolate Tahini Brownie Bites

Makes 12 brownie bites

High-heat oil, for greasing

½ cup tahini

1 large egg

2 teaspoons vanilla extract

3 tablespoons avocado oil

6 tablespoons coconut sugar

¼ teaspoon fine-grain sea salt

½ teaspoon baking soda

2 tablespoons unsweetened cocoa powder

Maldon or other flaky sea salt, for sprinkling

1 teaspoon instant espresso powder

¼ cup high-quality dark chocolate chips (see Tip, page 211)

TIP: If you don't like tahini, you can make this recipe with your favorite nut or seed butter—almond, peanut, cashew, and sunflower are all delicious!

Tahini, a Middle Eastern sesame seed paste, has a rich, almost bitter flavor that adds a sophisticated note to balance chocolate's creamy sweetness. Sesame seeds are higher in protein than other nuts and seeds, making this a blood sugar–balancing, super-filling dessert. They're rich in minerals and fats that make your skin glow, *and* a great choice for people with tree nut allergies. Here, the tahini and chocolate become brownie bites, the "oops, all edges" versions of brownies, which makes them even more perfect, in my eyes—but if you want more traditional squares, double the recipe, use a parchment-lined 8 × 8 pan, and bake for about 20 minutes, until a toothpick comes out clean.

1. Preheat the oven to 375°F. Lightly grease 12 cups of a mini muffin tin.

2. In a medium bowl, stir together the tahini, egg, vanilla, avocado oil, coconut sugar, salt, and baking soda until smooth. Transfer one-third of the batter to a small bowl. Stir the cocoa powder and espresso powder into the remaining batter in the medium bowl. Stir the chocolate chips into the chocolate batter.

3. Spoon 2 teaspoons of the chocolate mixture into each muffin cup, and push it to 1 side. Fill the remaining part with 1 teaspoon of the tahini mixture. Each muffin cup should be about two-thirds full. Tap the muffin tin gently on the countertop to settle the batter, then sprinkle the tops with the Maldon salt.

4. Bake for 10 to 15 minutes, or until a knife inserted into the center comes out clean. Let the brownie bites cool for at least 15 minutes in the pan before removing. Store in a tightly sealed container at room temperature for up to 5 days.

Salted Caramel Crack Popcorn

Makes 8 cups

¼ cup plus 2 tablespoons coconut oil

¼ cup unpopped popcorn kernels

½ cup raw cashews, gently crushed or chopped into chunks

½ cup maple syrup

1 teaspoon vanilla extract

¼ teaspoon fine-grain sea salt

¼ teaspoon baking soda

½ teaspoon Maldon salt

TIP: This recipe makes a softer caramel corn. If you have a bit more patience and want it crispy, like the ballpark classic, preheat the oven to 200°F. Spread your salted caramel–coated popcorn and cashews onto a parchment-lined baking sheet in a single layer, then bake for 1 hour, stirring and breaking up the popcorn every 20 minutes. Let it cool completely before storing in a tightly sealed container at room temperature.

Yes, this recipe is a riff on the classic baseball snack, but whether you take it out to the ball game or just eat it by the fistful at home, it is so, so good. Popcorn, despite its reputation as a treat, is actually a high-fiber, unprocessed whole grain. It's super-filling, and even more so here, tossed with heart-healthy cashews. The baking soda helps aerate the rich, vanilla-y caramel sauce, making it light and fluffy so it perfectly coats and crisps the popcorn. If you're making this with a partner, have one of you pop the popcorn and toast the cashews while the other makes the caramel sauce—although both of you should watch when you add the baking soda to the maple syrup mix; it foams up like crazy!

1. In the 2 tablespoons of coconut oil, pop the popcorn using the instructions on page 129. Remove the pot from the heat and immediately transfer the popcorn to a large bowl.

2. Place the cashews in a large skillet and toast, stirring, over medium-low heat, until golden brown, about 5 minutes. Add the cashews to the popcorn and gently toss to distribute.

3. Melt the remaining ¼ cup coconut oil in a medium pot over medium-high heat. Stir in the maple syrup, vanilla, and salt, and bring to a boil, continuing to stir occasionally. When it reaches a boil, allow the mixture to cook without stirring, for 4 minutes, or until it reaches 240°F (soft-ball stage in candy making). Stir in the baking soda.

4. Drizzle the caramel over the popcorn-and-cashew mixture, using a spoon to gently toss.

5. Pour the popcorn out onto a parchment-lined baking sheet, then sprinkle generously with the Maldon. Let cool slightly (the mixture will harden as it cools) before serving. Store in a tightly sealed container at room temperature for up to 4 days.

CBD-Infused Lavender Truffles

Makes about 30 truffles

FOR THE TRUFFLES

12 ounces high-quality dark chocolate, finely chopped

3 tablespoons coconut oil

1 cup canned full-fat coconut milk

2 tablespoons dried culinary lavender

1 teaspoon vanilla extract

¼ teaspoon ground cinnamon

240 mg unflavored CBD oil

OPTIONAL TOPPINGS

Flaky sea salt

Cacao powder

Ground cinnamon

Crushed almonds

If you have insomnia, inflammation, or anxiety, listen up: CBD, or cannabidiol, is about to become your new best friend. CBD is found in hemp and marijuana plants, but, unlike THC compounds, it doesn't get you high (and is legal in most states). It interacts with cannabinoid receptors all over your body and has been shown in a number of studies to quell inflammation and significantly ease insomnia and anxiety (in addition to more intensely therapeutic uses, like combating seizures in epileptic children). My friend Gretchen wrote a book about it (*CBD Oil: Everyday Secrets*), and we'll often get together on Sundays and make calming treats to eat throughout the week. Here it goes to the next level when combined with soothing lavender and creamy chocolate. If you want to make the recipe slightly easier, roll the refrigerated truffles in cacao powder, cinnamon, or nuts instead of coating them with chocolate (although I do think the contrast of hard shell and creamy interior is utterly delightful). Store these in your fridge and eat one whenever you're feeling stressed, or a craving for chocolate hits.

1. Combine 8 ounces of chocolate and 2 tablespoons of coconut oil in a large bowl.

2. Combine the coconut milk, lavender, vanilla, and cinnamon in a blender, and blend until mostly smooth. Transfer to a small pot. Cover and place over low heat to warm for 10 minutes. Strain the coconut milk mixture through a fine-mesh strainer set over a liquid measuring cup. Pour about half of the coconut milk mixture into the chocolate and coconut oil mixture and stir until smooth. Add a bit more milk at a time, stirring until smooth, until all the milk is incorporated. Stir in the CBD oil. Refrigerate for 3 to 4 hours, until the mixture reaches the texture of fudge.

(recipe continues)

3. Place 2 metal spoons or a melon baller in the freezer for 2 minutes to chill. Line a baking sheet with parchment paper. Use the chilled spoons to form the chilled chocolate mixture into small balls, about the size of cherries. Place the balls on the prepared baking sheet. Either roll the truffles in toppings, so they're finished now (as mentioned in the headnote), or place them in the freezer to chill again before coating.

4. Melt together the remaining 4 ounces of chocolate and 1 tablespoon coconut oil in a double boiler or in the microwave until homogenous, 1 to 3 minutes, stirring at 20-second intervals. Let cool for a minute or so and then, one at a time, place each truffle on a fork and dunk it into the melted chocolate, allowing any excess to drip off before returning the truffles to the baking sheet.

5. Top the truffles with whatever you desire (or leave them naked), and store in the fridge or freezer until you're ready to eat them. The truffles will last for 2 weeks in an airtight container in the fridge or up to 6 months in the freezer.

TIP: It can be tricky to navigate the nascent world of CBD suppliers. The most reputable supplier, in my opinion, is CW Hemp, which uses whole hemp extract, a slightly more whole-food form of CBD. You can order it online (it comes in several different strengths and flavors).

Mexican Hot Chocolate with Cinnamon Vanilla Bean Marshmallows

Serves 2

FOR THE MARSHMALLOWS

1½ tablespoons gelatin from grass-fed cows

½ cup honey

⅛ teaspoon fine-grain sea salt

1 teaspoon vanilla extract

1 teaspoon ground cinnamon

FOR THE HOT CHOCOLATE

2 cups nondairy milk

6 tablespoons raw cacao powder

2 teaspoons vanilla extract

2 teaspoons ground cinnamon

½ teaspoon chili powder

¼ teaspoon cayenne pepper

2 tablespoons maple syrup

Generous pinch of finely ground black pepper

Generous pinch of fine-grain sea salt

TIP: If you don't have a candy thermometer, be super-mindful of the marshmallows' cooking time. Remove the pot from the heat exactly 7 minutes after the mixture begins to simmer.

Mexican hot chocolate—that is, hot chocolate with cinnamon and spices—is one of my favorite drinks, and actually, all-around flavor combinations. In this version, you get to make your own marshmallows, which is shockingly simple. Your homemade version will include the added bonus of gelatin from grass-fed cows, a protein-rich superfood that helps seal your gut lining, decreasing inflammation. This means, essentially, that you can tell people the marshmallows are medicine and eat as many as you'd like! And they'll keep in a tightly sealed container at room temperature for up to a month. If you're making this with a partner, one of you can make the hot chocolate while the other handles the marshmallows.

1. **Make the marshmallows:** Line a 10 × 5-inch loaf pan with parchment paper, so it overhangs the long edges by about an inch. In a large bowl, sprinkle the gelatin over ¼ cup of water and whisk gently with a fork to combine. Set aside to bloom for at least 10 minutes, or up to 20.

2. Combine the honey, another ¼ cup of water, and the salt in a small pot fitted with a candy thermometer. Place the pot over medium heat and bring to a simmer, then reduce the heat to low and cook for 7 minutes, or until the mixture reaches 240°F (see Tip).

3. Using a stand mixer fitted with a whisk attachment or an electric mixer, beat the gelatin on medium while you drizzle in the honey mixture. Add the vanilla and cinnamon, and beat on high until the mixture is white and fluffy with soft peaks. Working very quickly, scrape the mixture into the prepared loaf pan and let it set for 2 to 3 hours at room temperature before cutting into 1½-inch squares with a sharp knife.

4. **Make the hot chocolate:** Heat the milk in a medium pot over medium heat until it's just about to boil, 3 to 5 minutes. Add the cacao, vanilla, cinnamon, chili, cayenne, maple syrup, black pepper, and salt, and whisk vigorously.

5. Divide the hot chocolate between 2 mugs, top with as many marshmallows as you'd like, and serve

Fun-Size Chocolate Nougat Candy Bars

Makes 15 mini candy bars

3 tablespoons melted cacao butter or coconut oil

2 tablespoons nondairy milk

1 tablespoon maple syrup

1 teaspoon vanilla extract

½ cup almond flour

⅛ teaspoon fine-grain sea salt

¼ cup chopped roasted peanuts or almonds

15 Medjool dates

1¼ cups dark chocolate chips or chopped dark chocolate

Maldon salt, for sprinkling

TIP: Cacao butter is the raw, cold-pressed oil from the cacao bean. It's used in chocolate bars and is filled with heart-healthy polyphenols. You can find it online or in most health food stores.

This recipe was inspired by my dad, who would always keep a bag of fun-size Snickers stashed in the freezer, should a candy emergency strike. I love candy, but I hate how time-consuming and finicky it is to make at home (not to mention the questionable ingredients), so I eliminated all of that. Instead, you'll whip up a healthy, almond-flour nougat, fold in some nuts, and shove that all inside a ripped open-date. Yes, a date—Mother Nature's caramel (she has a sweet tooth, too!). Packed with fiber and minerals, these treats take on a gooey quality that'll 100 percent satisfy any candy crisis.

1. Line a baking sheet with parchment paper.

2. In a medium bowl, mix together 2 tablespoons of cacao butter, the milk, maple syrup, vanilla, almond flour, and salt until well combined. Stir in the nuts.

3. Tear each date open lengthwise and remove the pit. Stuff each date with a spoonful of filling, then close them up as best you can (it's okay if they don't seal completely) before placing them on the prepared baking sheet. Place the dates in the freezer for at least 10 minutes.

4. Melt together the chocolate and the remaining 1 tablespoon of cacao butter in a double boiler or the microwave until homogenous, 1 to 3 minutes, stirring at 20-second intervals. Dip each date in the chocolate, using a spoon to turn to coat completely. Return the coated dates to the baking sheet and sprinkle them with the Maldon salt.

5. Chill in the fridge until the chocolate is set, about 1 hour (or 40 minutes in the freezer). These will keep in a sealed container in the fridge for a week, or in the freezer for up to 6 months.

The Everything Crisp

Makes one 8-inch crisp,
Serves 2–4

FOR THE FILLING

7 cups (¾-inch pieces) fruit of choice

1 tablespoon vanilla extract

2 tablespoons fresh lemon juice

2 tablespoons arrowroot powder

¼ teaspoon fine-grain sea salt

FOR THE TOPPING

5 tablespoons cold unsalted butter
from grass-fed cows, ghee, or
coconut oil

1 cup rolled oats

½ cup coconut sugar

½ cup almond flour

1 teaspoon vanilla extract

¼ teaspoon fine-grain salt

One of my favorite things to do with friends is fruit picking, whether it's apples in the fall or berries in the summer. When we get home, I immediately make a crisp, and we all gather around the table to eat it together, reveling in what amazing harvesters we are. This is my absolute favorite crisp recipe, and it can be used for almost any fruit: apples, blueberries, peaches, strawberries . . . (I beseech you to use common sense, though: grapes and bananas would be weird). I've also suggested a few more outside-the-box flavor variations in case you're high on that fresh-picked feeling and want to go crazy.

1. Preheat the oven to 350°F. Lightly grease an 8-inch pie plate or a cast-iron skillet.

2. Make the filling: In a large bowl, toss together the chopped fruit, vanilla, lemon juice, arrowroot, sea salt, and any additional flavorings (see page 225) until well coated. Transfer the filling to the prepared pie plate.

3. Make the topping: Wipe out the bowl, then chop the butter into small pieces and add it to the bowl, with the oats, coconut sugar, almond flour, vanilla, salt, and any additional flavorings (see page 225). Pinch it all together with your fingertips until it forms a shaggy, sandy dough. Sprinkle the topping evenly over the filling.

4. Bake for 45 minutes to 1 hour, or until the filling bubbles (or, in the case of apples and pears, is fork-tender) and the topping is golden brown but not burnt. Serve.

STRAWBERRY ROSEMARY

Use strawberries as your fruit of choice. Mix ⅓ teaspoon freshly ground black pepper into the filling. Mix 1 tablespoon minced fresh rosemary into the topping.

BLUEBERRY LAVENDER

Use blueberries as your fruit of choice. Use a mortar and pestle or the bottom of a glass to crush 1 tablespoon culinary lavender until powdery, before adding to the topping mixture.

APPLE CINNAMON

Use apples as your fruit of choice. Mix ¼ teaspoon ground cinnamon and a pinch of ground nutmeg into the filling. Mix ¼ teaspoon ground cardamom into the topping.

RASPBERRY BASIL

Use raspberries as your fruit of choice. Mix 2 tablespoons minced fresh basil into the filling.

Raspberry White Chocolate Moon Milk

Serves 2

2 tablespoons cacao butter or coconut oil, melted

2 cups nondairy milk

½ cup fresh or frozen raspberries

2 teaspoons rose water

2 teaspoons honey or maple syrup

Pinch of fine-grain sea salt

2 teaspoons powdered ashwagandha (optional)

2 teaspoons unflavored collagen powder (optional)

Moon milk comes from an Ayurvedic concept that's become trendy lately, based on the notion that nipping a warm, milky beverage before bed calms the nervous system, readying it for sleep. I personally love it because it provides just enough sweetness to curb my post-dinner sugar cravings, while upping the ante with a few additional sleep-inducing ingredients: ashwagandha, an adaptogen that's been shown to reduce anxiety, and collagen powder, which signals the body to release melatonin, a hormone that tells your body it's time to turn off. Sweet dreams!

Combine the cacao butter, milk, and raspberries in a small pot over medium heat, and warm until almost boiling, 3 to 5 minutes. Let it cool until you can touch it without burning your finger, about 3 minutes, then transfer it to a blender. Add the rose water, honey, salt, and, if desired, the ashwagandha and collagen. Blend until the mixture is very smooth. Pour into 2 mugs and sip immediately.

TIP: With adaptogens, it's important to take care to find a high-quality supplier to avoid contaminants and mislabeling. I like Mountain Rose Herbs and Sun Potion, both of which are available online.

Honey-Rose Rice Pudding with Pistachio-Cardamom Crumble

Serves 2

⅓ cup uncooked medium-grain white rice

1 (13.5-ounce) can full-fat coconut milk

¼ teaspoon fine-grain sea salt

2 tablespoons honey

1 teaspoon vanilla extract

1 teaspoon rose water

1 tablespoon chia seeds

¼ cup raw, shelled pistachios, roughly chopped

¼ teaspoon ground cardamom

Rice pudding is one of the best, and more underrated desserts, in my opinion. But how do you make it better for you? The secret is combining it with chia pudding, a health world staple that's good for your gut, filled with healthy fats and protein, and the secret to having the best poop ever (sorry, but it's true). Here it makes the rice pudding vegan (an added bonus that lets you share it with a Healthier Together partner of any dietary preference), but also gives it a stick-to-your-ribs satisfaction without being at all heavy. The mix of rose, pistachio, and cardamom is one of my favorite flavor combinations.

1. Combine the rice, coconut milk, ½ cup of water and ⅛ teaspoon of salt in a medium, heavy-bottomed pot. Bring to a boil over medium-high heat, stirring often, then reduce the heat to low, cover, and simmer for 20 minutes, until the rice is fully cooked but there is still liquid remaining. Remove the pot from the heat and let the mixture cool for 10 to 15 minutes, then stir in 1 tablespoon of honey, the vanilla, rose water, and chia seeds. Let sit for 10 minutes, until the chia seeds soak up the additional liquid and it becomes rice pudding–like in texture.

2. At this point, you can proceed with warm pudding, or chill the pudding in the fridge. It will keep, covered, for up to a week.

3. When you're ready to serve, add the pistachios and cardamom to a small skillet over low heat and toast, stirring occasionally, until fragrant and the pistachios are just beginning to turn golden brown, about 5 minutes. Add the remaining 1 tablespoon of honey and ⅛ teaspoon of salt. Stir well to coat, then remove the pan from the heat.

4. Top the pudding with the warm pistachio crumble and serve.

Healthier Together
21-Day Cleanup

I think the best detox is all about supporting your body to detoxify *itself* with the ample tools it has available. This cleanup is designed to reset your taste buds, help eliminate your sugar cravings, boost your energy, and flood your system with vegetable goodness to nourish every one of your cells. Your skin will be clearer, your belly will be flatter, and you won't feel at all deprived. And the best part? Doing it with a partner makes you much more likely to stick to it—and enjoy yourself in the process. So pick a buddy (see Pick a Partner, page 14, for some tips on how to do it with anyone, anywhere) and dive in!

The guidelines:

- Drink one huge glass of room-temperature water when you wake up every morning. We wake up super dehydrated, so rehydrating first thing sets up your system for success.

- Drink water and herbal tea throughout the day. Try not to consume caffeine after 3 p.m. and stick to plain coffee, matcha, and green and black tea. (If you're willing to give up caffeine altogether, even better.)

- Avoid alcohol during the cleanup to give your liver, your body's primary detox organ, a break. If you don't want to abstain altogether, keep it to two alcoholic beverages a week and choose the healthier options on page 134.

- Stay away from refined sugar altogether and limit unrefined sugar (other than fruit) to the days of the plan when you're also having dessert.

- Move your body throughout the day as much as possible. It's not great to do high-intensity workouts when you're detoxing, and the jury is still out on how much that type of exercise negatively impacts your hormones in the long run (some research shows that the spiking cortisol of super-sweaty sessions leads to *more* belly fat). That said, you still want to move your body regularly and constantly. Try not to sit for more than an hour at a time, peppering your day with walks and gentle stretching. Park in the farthest spot in the lot. Walk or bike to work. When you do "work out," try to do something recreational: hit some tennis balls with your Healthier Together partner, or go for a hike and soak in nature.

- Take a daily probiotic. This helps quell sugar cravings and rebalance your gut bacteria, especially when paired with potent prebiotics like the Fully Loaded Baked Potato-less Soup (page 66). I like the brands Garden of Life and Seed probiotics.

Day 1

- Green smoothie of choice (page 166)
- Moroccan-ish Sunset Salad (page 109)
- Pumpkin and Rosemary Savory Porridge with Sautéed Mushrooms (page 27)

Day 2

- Green smoothie of choice (page 166)
- 10-Minute Poke Bowl (made with beet option) (page 38)
- Broccoli Rice Tabbouleh with Lemon and Dill (page 115)

Day 3

- Green smoothie of choice (page 166)
- Kombucha-Miso Massaged Kale Salad with Spicy Quinoa (page 119)
- Fully Loaded Baked Potato-less Soup (with no cheese or coconut bacon) (page 66)

Day 4

- Green smoothie of choice (page 166).
- Chopped Thai Satay Salad (page 41)
- Chicken and Butternut Squash Tikka Masala (made with chickpea option) (page 79)

Day 8

- Green smoothie of choice (page 166)
- Kombucha-Miso Massaged Kale Salad with Spicy Quinoa (page 119)
- Carrot Tartare with Crispy Capers and Super-Seeded Rosemary Crackers (page 185)

Day 9

- Green smoothie of choice (page 166)
- Chopped Thai Satay Salad (page 41)
- Immune-Boosting Turmeric Golden Milk Daal (page 120)

Day 10

- Green smoothie of choice (page 166)
- Frozen Broccoli & Basil Soup with Sweet and Spicy Cashews (page 30)
- 10-Minute Poke Bowl (made with beet option) (page 38)

Day 11

- Green smoothie of choice (page 166)
- Broccoli Rice Tabbouleh with Lemon and Dill (page 115)
- Turmeric-Tahini Whole Roasted Cauliflower with Spiced Sweet Potato Lentils (page 191)

Day 15

- Green smoothie of choice (page 166)
- Broccoli Rice Tabbouleh with Lemon and Dill (page 115)
- Roasted Cauliflower and Crispy Chickpeas with Golden Ghee Dressing (page 123)

Day 16

- Green smoothie of choice (page 166)
- Kombucha-Miso Massaged Kale Salad with Spicy Quinoa (page 119)
- Carrot Tartare with Crispy Capers and Super-Seeded Rosemary Crackers (page 185)

Day 17

- Green smoothie of choice (page 166)
- Chopped Thai Satay Salad (page 41)
- Warm Winter Vegetable Salad with Maple-Cranberry Vinaigrette (page 116)

Day 18

- Green smoothie of choice (page 166)
- 10-Minute Poke Bowl (made with beet option) (page 38)
- *Actually* Delicious Green Detox Soup with Toasted Hemp Gremolata (page 106)

Day 5

- Green smoothie of choice (page 166)
- *Actually* Delicious Green Detox Soup with Toasted Hemp Gremolata (page 106)
- Roasted Cauliflower and Crispy Chickpeas with Golden Ghee Dressing (page 123)

Day 6

- Green smoothie of choice (page 150)
- Frozen Broccoli and Basil Soup with Sweet and Spicy Cashews (page 30)
- Immune-Boosting Turmeric Golden Milk Daal (page 120)

Day 7

- Green smoothie of choice (page 166)
- Warm Winter Vegetable Salad with Maple-Cranberry Vinaigrette (page 116)
- Zucchini Latkes with Apple-Rosemary Compote (page 58)
- Sweet treat of choice

Day 12

- Green smoothie of choice (page 166)
- Fully Loaded Baked Potato-less Soup (with no cheese or coconut bacon) (page 66)
- Sweet Potato Tostada with Refried Black Beans & Creamy Pepita Cilantro Sauce (page 112)

Day 13

- Green smoothie of choice (page 166)
- Moroccan-ish Sunset Salad (page 109)
- Caramelized Parsnip Steaks with Zesty Chimichurri Sauce (page 178)

Day 14

- Green smoothie of choice (page 166)
- Ginger-Basil Bone Broth Ramen (page 103)
- Chicken and Butternut Squash Tikka Masala with Super-Fresh Mint Cilantro Chutney (made with chickpea option) (page 79)
- Sweet treat of choice

Day 19

- Green smoothie of choice (page 166)
- Ginger-Basil Bone Broth Ramen (page 103)
- Zucchini Latkes with Apple-Rosemary Compote (page 58)

Day 20

- Green smoothie of choice (page 166)
- Frozen Broccoli and Basil Soup with Sweet and Spicy Cashews (page 30)
- Chicken and Butternut Squash Tikka Masala with Super-Fresh Mint Cilantro Chutney (made with chickpea option) (page 79)

Day 21

- Green smoothie of choice (page 166)
- Immune-Boosting Turmeric Golden Milk Daal (page 120)
- *Actually* Delicious Green Detox Soup with Toasted Hemp Gremolata (page 106)
- Sweet treat of choice

Acknowledgments

It's so gratifying to write a book about how much easier—and better—it is to go through life with other people, because the support of my community has been a favorite and formative element in my own story.

Zack, I literally didn't eat vegetables when I met you. Who would've guessed that someday I'd be penning a healthy cookbook? You've made me healthier in all of the obvious ways, but far more important, in the ways beyond eating well that typically slip the mind. I'm healthier because you stretch my mind with fascinating conversations. I'm healthier because you make me play sports when I'd otherwise just be reading. I'm healthier because of our travels, and because of how you help me relieve my stress, and how you make me laugh. At my core, I'm healthier because you make me so much happier, and I'm so grateful to get to go on this journey with you. I can't imagine writing this book or any book without you, and I appreciate every single second of time and energy you've put into both it and me.

Papa, you've helped me test so many of these recipes. Whether you're completely botching asparagus soup or developing an addiction to the Salted Caramel Crack Popcorn, your feedback emails were often the highlight of my day. You were one of my first Healthier Together partners—you were, in fact, the person who first introduced me to what food could be, from our Chez Panisse café dinners to the Thai food in Chicago. You don't support me with only words but action, and I recognize how rare and magical it is to have someone like you in my life.

Mom, it's been so wonderful to see you take an interest in my food, even when you'd probably be happy eating soup for the rest of your life. I love how open you are to changing your diet and lifestyle (and still consider getting you to eat fat one of my biggest wins!). Thank you so much for endlessly championing this book, and my writing career generally.

To my second family: Susan and Leslie. From recipe testing (if Leslie likes it, it's basically golden) to helping foster my cooking career in its nascent stages on Rock Lane, I feel in so many ways like I couldn't have gotten where I am today without your unwavering support.

Amanda, you're one of a kind. To have such a power woman behind my books is such a privilege, and one that I appreciate daily. I couldn't have dreamt up a better editor. To the rest of my Potter team—Elora, Natasha, Mia, Gabrielle, Kim—you do beautiful work, but you're also just some of the most fun, interesting, kick-ass people I've had the pleasure of knowing. It makes me want to write more books just so I have more excuses to talk to you.

To my agent, Alia, who has endured far too many of my emotional phone calls. You're such a wise and giving person, and you've gone so above and beyond in helping me not only as an author, but as a human. We started with *Glow Pops* and now we're here, and I can't wait to see where we go next together.

To Lauren, Mariana, and Maeve: I'm so glad we were able to reunite the gang for this book! Our week of shooting was one of the best weeks of my life—it made me want to write a million more cookbooks, just to bask in more of that powerful, women-led energy. I love you all and the fact that you created photos more beautiful than I can imagine is only a bonus.

To my recipe-testing gang: Morgan, Nancy, Katie, Aunt Joan, Chiara, Amber, Elizabeth, Chloe, Gabrielle, Catherine, Kristin, Christine, Emily, Abdul, Erin, Emma, Jenna, and Leigh, you've all made this book so much better. Thank you for your incredible feedback—this book would literally not be the same without you.

I believe that community is one of the least appreciated and most important pillars of wellness, and so many of my friends and family have supported me not just on this book but throughout my life. It would take years to thank all of you for your work in shaping me, but know that it's so appreciated. On this book particularly, Stacy, I can't believe how many hours you willingly dedicated to hanging out in my kitchen, listening to *Hamilton* and testing different types of miso in soup. Ben, your frank and honest feedback and willingness to use your new Vitamix to take recipes for a spin was so appreciated. Gretchen, you cooked with me and ate with me and laughed with me and helped me stay sane throughout this whole process. Hogan, you answered my urgent cooking questions, no matter what strange time of day I called. Elizabeth, from connecting me to my

favorite recipe tester to hanging out with me while I eschewed any semblance of a social life to cook to making me feel extremely confident about the Brussels sprout tacos, your presence made this book so much more fun. Katie, I've loved bonding with you over our love for food. I'm so happy to have you as a sister and can't wait to see where our relationship goes from here.

My mindbodygreen community has provided me with so much more than an office and a job here in Brooklyn. You guys are my family; our office is my home. I feel so immensely lucky to go to work every day with so many brilliant people whom I love dearly, and do work that's both fun and world-changing. Thank you to all of you.

Finally, to my readers at mindbodygreen and lizmoody.com: I've so enjoyed getting to know you throughout the years. I never lose sight of the fact that it is because of you that I get to do what I do, so to you I say: Thank you, thank you, thank you. I like to think we're all a big, Healthier Together family, and that brings a big ol' grin to my face.

Index

About the Author

Liz Moody spent years traveling the world as a
newspaper columnist before settling in Brooklyn, where
she lives in a tiny apartment with her husband (and
main Healthier Together partner), Zack. She is currently
the food director at mindbodygreen, one of the world's
leading wellness websites, and her work has been
featured in *Vogue, Cosmopolitan, goop,* and more. In
2017, she published her first cookbook, *Glow Pops*, with
Clarkson Potter. For more healthy recipes and general
wellness musings, visit her at lizmoody.com or on
Instagram @lizmoody.